LaDy BUg & FRIENDS QUILTS

by Quilted Frog

Carla Scott & Leanne Smith

 American Quilter's Society

P. O. Box 3290 • Paducah, KY 42002-3290
www.AmericanQuilter.com

D1315054

 Includes CD with printable patterns

Located in Paducah, Kentucky, the American Quilter's Society (AQS) is dedicated to promoting the accomplishments of today's quilters. Through its publications and events, AQS strives to honor today's quiltmakers and their work and to inspire future creativity and innovation in quiltmaking.

Executive Book Editor: Andi Milam Reynolds
Editor: Linda Baxter Lasco
Copy Editor: Chrystal Abhalter
Graphic Design: Quilted Frog
AQS Graphic Designer: Lynda Smith
Cover Design: Michael Buckingham
Photography: Avion Photo and Red Ashton Photograpbhy
         Alternative LadyBug Pillow Case: Charles R. Lynch

Additional copies of this book may be ordered from the American Quilter's Society, PO Box 3290, Paducah, KY 42002-3290, or online at www.AmericanQuilter.com.

© 2011, Quilted Frog
Publication and distribution rights, AQS
Library of Congress Cataloging-in-Publication Data

Scott, Carla.
  Ladybug & friends quilts / by Carla Scott & Leanne Smith.
    p. cm.
  ISBN 978-1-57432-684-0
  1. Quilting--Patterns. 2. Appliqué--Patterns. 3. Patchwork quilts.
I. Smith, Leanne. II. Title. III. Title: Ladybug and friends quilts.
TT779.S363 2011
  746.46--dc22
             2011006911

DEDICATION

We'd like to dedicate this book to our parents, William and Alice Faye McCarl. They encouraged creativity in all we did, taught us to draw and sew, and provided materials for all our projects. In addition, we want to thank our husbands, Howard Scott and Rock Smith. We could never have been the Quilted Frog without their support.

CONTENTS

The CD includes:

All the pattern files, which have been formatted to print on your home printer. You will print out the pattern pages & tape them together. It's easy, fast & accurate.

Large format files, which have been included for printing professionally on 36" wide paper. Be sure to check patterns for accuracy before using them.

Adobe® Reader® installers for PC & Mac computers. You will need this easy to install PDF file reader to open the patterns on your computer.

How to use the CD

If you are working on a Windows® computer, just insert the CD in your computer. The CD has been designed to automatically open the folder containing the files for printing the pattern pieces.

If you use a Mac® computer, an icon of the CD will appear on your desktop. Just double click on the CD icon then double click on the ladybugpatterns folder to access the pattern files.

To install Adobe Reader software, Windows users will need to double click on the My Computer icon on your desktop then double click on the Ladybug & Friends CD icon. Open the Install Reader folder. The installer file you need will be inside the Windows folder. Just double click on the AdbeRdr708_en_US.exe file to install Adobe Reader on your computer.

To install Adobe Reader software, Mac users will need to double click on the the Ladybug & Friends CD icon on your desktop then double click on the Install Reader folder. The installer file you need will be inside the Mac folder. Just double click on the Acrobat Reader Installer to install Adobe Reader on your computer.

INTRODUCTION

Once we were two little frogs living in a lovely three-bedroom pond in the Arizona desert. Our names were Carla and Leanne and because we were little frogs our parents lived with us, too. Mother frog was an enchanted seamstress. She made her little frogs beautiful clothes and taught us to sew as well. Father frog was an artist. He could paint or sculpt or photograph anything. He let his little frogs experiment with paint and clay and papier-mâché. So of course we had lots of fun making any and everything we could think of. Making was our favorite thing to do.

Over the years of making things we grew from little frogs to grown-up frogs. Carla loved painting and clay and glass so she ran companies that made wonderful treasures of glass and porcelain. She sold her treasures all over the world and created collectibles for Disney and Warner Brothers. Carla lived in ponds from Arizona to California to Texas. Leanne thought cameras and photography were best of all. She photographed mountains and people and brides and animals. Leanne stayed in an Arizona pond just a few miles from the original three-bedroom pond. And all the time the frogs have been sewing and quilting and making and making and making.

One day long after we had married and had little frogs of our own, we were together in Arizona because Carla had a new little grand-frog. We wanted to make something together just like when we were little frogs. What would we make? A quilt. A quilt with chickens. And so our very first Quilted Frog quilt came to be. And what was that quilt? The Little Red Hen. Like most mother frogs we could really relate to a story about a mother who did the work all by herself!

After that first quilt we had so many ideas we decided to call ourselves the Quilted Frog and make our whimsical designs into patterns for other quilters. We love bright colors and graphic designs. We love the way that fusible appliqué lets us "paint" with fabric. As we worked on our designs we decided that adding bold black outlines would give our quilts a little extra pop. So we created our Easy OutLine Appliqué technique. Because each line is traced by hand and then cut by hand it looks hand drawn. We loved our new technique and we think you will, too. Easy OutLine Appliqué is so simple that anyone who can cut paper dolls can make Quilted Frog quilts.

So here we are after years of patterns and quilts and shows and contests with our very first book.

All the basic information and techniques are grouped together in the front of the book. The designs with their materials lists, cutting measurements, and specific directions follow the basics in several groups of related projects. All of the projects are easy enough for beginning quilters. The adorable designs and little extras will keep experienced quilters happy and interested from start to finish. We like pieced backgrounds with borders and corner details so our patterns walk you through making those. But all of our appliqué designs are complete in themselves. If you don't like to piece quilts or don't really sew just make the easy appliqués and fuse them to a single piece of fabric cut to the project's finished dimensions.

We think this book has something for everyone. Any of the pillowcase designs and the MONSTER TOTE BAG can be made in an evening or a weekend. You could even add our pillowcase appliqués to a store-bought pillowcase. The BABY QUILT is the smallest and quickest of the quilts. The LADYBUG QUILT and the CAR QUILT are just as easy to piece but they will require a few more evenings to make the appliqués. Spend some more time making all of the LadyBug or Car projects and you can decorate a child's room. If you are looking for a project that requires no sewing before you quilt it, the CAR GROWTH CHART is entirely fusible appliqué. There is no piecing at all.

We had fun planning creating these designs for you. Now we hope you will have fun making them. We made the projects with the bright colors we love. Now you can make each design your own by choosing the colors you love. When you are done you can keep the quilts for yourself or give them to the little frogs or chickens or ducks or fish that you love!

Happy Quilting,

Carla & Leanne

Quilted Frog

BASIC NINE-PATCH QUILT PATTERN

The finished size varies according to how many blocks and rows you make.

Quilting can be a lot of fun for beginners and experienced quilters if you stick to the basics and keep it simple. Using a simple pattern frees you to experiment with fabrics and appliqués. Add borders and appliqués to a simple quilt pattern and it will look different every time you make it. There are three quilts in this book and all three are made from a simple pattern that alternates Nine-Patch blocks with blocks of a single fabric. We rely on pretty fabric, different borders, and whimsical appliqués to make each quilt something special. A Nine-Patch quilt is a good first quilt for brand new quilters and a great canvas for experienced quilters to decorate. It's a chameleon pattern that you can make a hundred different ways.

There are two types of blocks in each of our Nine-Patch quilt patterns—Block 1 is a square of a single fabric and Block 2 is a pieced Nine-Patch block. Look at the pictures of the quilts to see how we changed the look of each quilt by using different fabrics and placing the lights and darks differently. Here are some basic guidelines for choosing fabrics for a Nine-Patch quilt.

For the single fabric squares almost anything works.

We like large prints like the floral we used in the Baby Quilt (page 61). Large prints make it look like you did elaborate piecing but it is so simple because you just used one fabric.

We love batiks and you can see how well the almost solid look of the batik works in the bright version of the LadyBug Quilt (page 24).

Small, busy prints like the crazy polka dot we used in the Car Quilt (page 45) make the whole quilt seem active and happy.

Tone on tone prints like the harlequin check we used in the brown and pink version of the LadyBug Quilt (page 25) make a calm background that doesn't distract from the chains that appear when you place the darkest fabric in the corners of the Nine-Patch blocks.

For the Nine-Patch blocks you need fabrics that contrast in color and value—the lightness or darkness of the color. Make your Nine-Patch blocks with the lighter color in the corners with a third color in the center and the blocks will appear to be flowers with four petals.

Make your Nine-Patch blocks with the darker color in the corners. Choose a center color that is similar to the dark color and when you sew the blocks together, you will see dark chains going diagonally across your quilt.

You can make each quilt truly your own by the fabrics you choose. So make a trip to your favorite fabric shop or go through your stash and gather some fabrics you love. Have fun experimenting with colors and print size. Use these basic directions to make your blocks. Then complete your quilt according to the directions for each individual design.

We suggest that you read all of these basic directions plus the directions for the design you have chosen before starting your quilt.

Unless otherwise noted, all strips are cut selvage to selvage across the width of the fabric.

Use ¼" seam allowance unless otherwise noted.

All of the blocks for the Nine-Patch quilts in this book measure 6½" x 6½" unfinished.

The example pictures in these directions show the fabrics from the Baby Quilt.

Block 1

Cut 6½" x 6½" squares from the strips.

The directions for the design you have chosen will tell you how many strips to cut and how many square blocks to cut from the strips.

Block 1 completed

Block 2—Nine Patch

Nine-Patch #1 Unit will always contain the fabric for the centers of the blocks.

Cut 2½" strips of Block 2 Fabric A.
Cut half as many 2½" strips of Block 2 Fabric C.

The directions for the design you have chosen will tell you which colors and how many strips to cut.

Sew a Fabric A strip to both sides of each Fabric C strip.

Press the seams toward Fabric A on all units. This will make your seams lock together when making the Nine-Patch blocks.

FABRIC A
FABRIC C
FABRIC A

Fabric A and Fabric C units completed

Cut 2½" segments from the Fabric A/Fabric C units. Each unit will make 16 segments.

Cuts from Fabric A—Fabric C units completed Nine–Patch #2 Unit

Cut 2½" strips of Block 2 Fabric B.
Cut half as many 2½" strips of Block 2 Fabric A.

The directions for the design you have chosen will tell you how many strips to cut and which colors to use for these units.

Sew a Fabric B strip to both sides of each Fabric A strip.

Press the seams toward Fabric A on all units. This will make your seams lock together when making the Nine-Patch blocks.

FABRIC B
FABRIC A
FABRIC B

Fabric B—Fabric A units completed

Cut 2½" segments from the Fabric B/Fabric A units. Each unit will make 16 segments.

Cuts from Fabric B—Fabric A units completed

Sew a B-A-B piece to both sides of each A-C-A piece to make complete Nine-Patch blocks.

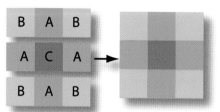

Block 2 completed

Sew the blocks together as shown to make rows of blocks. Press the seams toward Block 1.

The directions for the design you have chosen will tell you how many blocks in each row and how many rows to make.

**Depending on the design you have chosen:

Some rows will start and end with a Nine-Patch block (Block 2).

Some rows will start and end with a single fabric block (Block 1).

Some rows will start with a Nine-Patch block (Block 2) and end with a single fabric block (Block 1).

Some rows may be like this.

Some rows may be like this.

Some rows may be like this.

Sew the rows of blocks together to make the main part of the quilt top.

Your quilt top will look similar to this.

Now that your quilt top is complete you are ready to add borders. Turn to the section on adding borders (page 15) and check the directions for your chosen design for the measurements.

BASIC PILLOWCASE PATTERN

Finished size approximately 21½" x 31½"

Visit our website at www.quiltedfrog.com/freetutorials/ for a video demonstration. While you are there you can join our fun new Pillowcase Club, www.quiltedfrog.com/shop/category/pillowcase-club/

Pillowcases are great evening, weekend, or stash buster projects. Making a pillowcase is a fun way to make an impressive finished item that requires minimal amounts of time and materials. They are perfect projects for beginners who want to try out basic quilting and appliqué skills. Experienced quilters will love the practically instant gratification and the opportunity to do detailed quilting on a small scale. Whether you make pillowcases for yourself or as gifts, you will love the designs we have included in this collection.

So pull out your favorite fat quarters and leftovers from other quilting projects and make one of our whimsical pillowcases. We like bright colors but the designs work equally well with a more muted color palette. We almost never use fabrics that are solid colors and you will find that subtle prints usually work better when making small projects like pillowcases. Look for fabrics that have some interesting variation but still read as basically one color.

Each pillowcase has three basic parts:
• The main part or body of the pillowcase
• The border or borders
• The appliquéd cuff

We will explain how to quilt the appliquéd part of the cuff just like in our samples. If that seems like too much work you can skip the quilting and just appliqué the cuff.

The instructions here will guide you through the basics of pillowcase construction. We suggest that you read all of these basic directions plus the directions for the design you have chosen before starting your pillowcase. Please note:

Some designs have multiple borders; the variations are explained with each project.

Piece the first cuff section if necessary before adding the appliqués and quilting.

To complete each pillowcase, refer to the detailed Easy OutLine Appliqué Technique.

All strips are cut selvage to selvage across the width of the fabric unless otherwise noted.

Use a ¼" seam allowance unless otherwise noted.

Appliqués

The example pictures in these directions show the fabrics from the FLOWER PILLOWCASE, which is available free at www.quiltedfrog.com/bonus/ to purchasers of this book.

Make all appliqués for the pillowcase design you have chosen. Refer to the Easy OutLine Appliqué Technique (pages 12–14) for complete directions on how to make the appliqués.

Remember that all appliqué patterns are printed in mirror image so the finished projects will be oriented like the sample projects.

After making all the appliqués remove the paper backing from the fusible.

Pillowcase Cuff

For each pillowcase, cut 3 pieces of the cuff fabric and label them Cuff A, Cuff B, and Cuff C.

• Cuff A is the front of the cuff. This is the piece you will appliqué and quilt. In some of the patterns Cuff A will be pieced. Cuff A will always be cut or pieced larger than its final size to allow for take-up during quilting. When placing appliqués, keep in mind that you will be trimming Cuff A so keep the appliqués away from the edges. If in doubt, cut a piece of paper to the finished Cuff A size. Make sure your appliqués will fit in that area before fusing them to the Cuff A piece.

• Cuff B is the outside back of the cuff. This is the piece you will sew to Cuff A after it is completed.

• Cuff C is the lining and is added to the bottom of the Cuff A/Cuff B unit. It will be folded to the inside of the cuff when the pillowcase is complete.

Cutting sizes are included with the directions for each pillowcase design.

Fabric widths can vary from 40"–44" wide. When making patterns that use the same fabric for all or part of the 3 cuff pieces, make certain you use no more than half the fabric width for Cuff A and Cuff B.

For example, if the pattern says:

Cut 1 strip 10" x 22" for Cuff A
and
Cut 1 strip 10" x 22" for Cuff B

your fabric needs to be at least 44" wide. If your fabric is narrower, adjust the width of the Cuff A and Cuff B pieces to half the width of the fabric OR buy an extra ¼ yard of the cuff fabric. Do not include the selvages as part of the width. The selvages are removed because they are usually different in color and weave from the rest of the fabric.

CENTER OF FABRIC (FOLD)

SELVAGE	**CUFF A** MUST FIT IN THIS SECTION OF THE FABRIC	**CUFF B** MUST FIT IN THIS SECTION OF THE FABRIC
	CUFF C MUST FIT IN THIS SECTION OF THE FABRIC	SELVAGE

Cut out Cuff A.

Place all of the appliqués on Cuff A. Refer to the pillowcase photo for placement. Fuse the appliqués in place following the fusible manufacturer's instructions.

Cut a piece of batting several inches larger than Cuff A. Layer Cuff A with the batting.

Pin or baste the 2 layers together and quilt by machine. If you choose not to quilt the cuff do not use the batting.

If you do not quilt the cuff it is a good idea to stitch around the edges of the appliqué shapes.

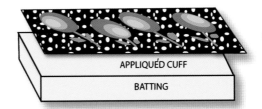

Use a variety of thread colors to add detail and dimension to the design on the cuff.

Add detail to the design with quilting.

Once the quilting is complete, trim Cuff A to the size listed in the pillowcase design directions.

Cut out Cuff B.

Place Cuff B and Cuff A right sides together. Sew one short end of the unquilted Cuff B to the quilted Cuff A.

Press the seam open.

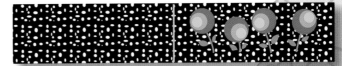

The yellow line indicates the seam.

Cut out Cuff C. See the specific design directions for the measurements of this piece.

Sew Cuff C to the bottom edge of the Cuff A/Cuff B unit.

Press the seam open.

Set the cuff unit aside.

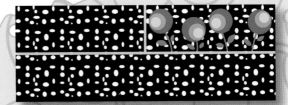

The yellow lines indicate the seams.

Pillowcase Body

Use your rotary cutter and ruler to square up the cut edges of the pillowcase body fabric.

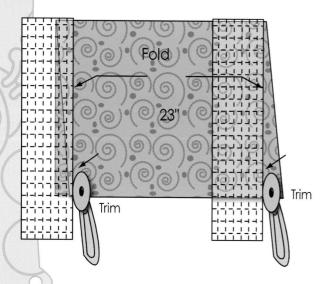

Border

Cut a border strip the width specified in the design instructions.

Sew the border piece to the top edge of the body. Press the seam toward the darker fabric.

Measure the width of the pillowcase body and the cuff unit. If necessary trim them to make sure they are the same width. This trimming will remove the selvages.

Try not to remove more fabric than necessary, in order to keep the pillowcase as wide as the fabric allows.

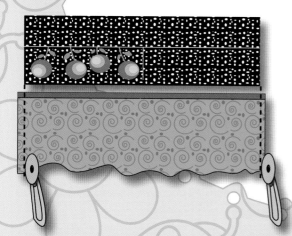

Trim edges if necessary so that cuff and body of pillowcase are the same width.

Fold the pillowcase body in half right sides together, matching the selvage-trimmed sides. Sew across the end opposite the border and along the side as shown.

With right sides together stitch edges together along dotted lines.

Serge or zigzag stitch the seam allowance if desired.

Turn the body section right-side out. Press flat.

Complete the cuff

Fold the cuff of the pillowcase in half across the width, right sides together. Sew along the short ends to form a tube.

Press the seam open.

Fold the cuff in half lengthwise along the seam between Cuff A/Cuff B and Cuff C, wrong sides together with the appliqué facing out.

Raw edges

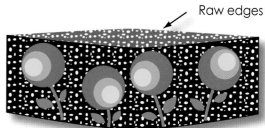

Baste the raw edges together by machine or hand.

Sew Cuff to Body

Turn the cuff tube so the appliqué (Cuff A) is on the inside.

Place the cuff tube over the top of the body right sides together, aligning the raw edges. The appliqués will be touching the right side of the body fabric.

Sew the raw edges together. Finish this seam so that it won't ravel. There are several ways to do this:

- Stitch the seam with a serger to create an overcast edge.

- Stitch the seam a second time with a zigzag or an overcast stitch that covers the raw edges of the fabrics.

With right sides together stitch raw edges together along dotted lines.

Turn the cuff right-side out and press the seam flat.

Your pillowcase is complete and ready to use.

EASY OUTLINE APPLIQUÉ TECHNIQUE

See www.quiltedfrog.com/freetutorials/ for a video demonstration.

We created the Easy OutLine Appliqué Technique for making detailed fusible appliqués with an appearance of being outlined by hand. The outlines help maintain the clarity of the pictures and add a little extra pop to the designs. Because our technique involves tracing and cutting each shape by hand, there are slight differences in the outline thickness. These differences are what give our technique its hand-drawn appearance. The variations in the outlines bring the designs to life and enhance their visual appeal. You know that your quilt will be truly unique as you choose fabrics and colors and create outlines that show the touch of your own hand.

At first glance our designs may seem complex, but don't worry. The technique is so simple that you will be able to achieve wonderful results on your very first Easy OutLine project. If you can cut paper dolls you can make a Quilted Frog appliqué design.

Gather all of the appliqué fabrics, your paper-backed fusible web, a sharp pencil, and a good pair of scissors. We recommend keeping all of the appliqué parts in a box or basket as you cut them. This keeps everything organized and together until you are ready to fuse the individual appliqué parts to the black base.

Make all the appliqué units using our Easy OutLine Appliqué Technique. Use the materials list and project photo for color placement. Use a lightweight paper-backed fusible web of your choice. Follow the manufacturer's instructions for fusing. Use a pressing cloth to protect your iron from glue residue. Use a Teflon® appliqué sheet on the ironing board when assembling appliqué units.

Here are some things to keep in mind as you make your appliqués:

Use a mechanical pencil to trace the patterns on the paper backing of the fusible web. The rough surface quickly wears down the pencil lead. Using a mechanical pencil makes it easier to keep a sharp point. For the examples in these directions, we used a red pen so that the lines show in the pictures. Whatever you use to trace

the designs, be certain it is permanent so it will not smear. **The appliqué patterns are printed in reverse of the finished project. This is so the pictures will face the right direction when you are finished.**

Fusing directions vary from product to product. To ensure success, always follow the instructions provided by the manufacturer of the fusible web you are using.

You must let your pieces cool before removing the paper backing. The paper backing of some fusible webs are easier to remove if you wait a few hours after ironing.

Trace the patterns carefully so your finished quilt will look like the original.

Cut the pieces out carefully. Your cutting will also influence the final appearance of your project.

If you plan to eliminate quilting or to quilt lightly over the appliqués, it is a good idea to stitch around the edges of each piece. For example, if you are grid quilting the entire quilt, the appliqués will need more stitching.

The appliqué patterns print with heavy black outlines. These heavy outlines will create the spaces that give your quilt the appearance of being outlined by hand. (See detailed printing instructions on pages 21–22.)

Number each section of the pattern. Note which pieces will be cut from the same fabric.

Fusible web paper–side up

Lay paper-backed fusible web paper-side up over the pattern page. To make a black silhouette for the appliqué base, trace around the complete shape of the design on the **OUTSIDE** edge of the heavy black outline. The black base shape you just traced creagtes the outlines in the finished appliques.The red line on the diagram shows where you will trace. The block base creates the outlines in the finished appliqué.

The video demonstration at www.quiltedfrog.com/freetutorials/ shows this.

The specific directions for each design will include a diagram showing how the base for the appliqués will look.

If one section of the picture touches another section of the picture, both sections are part of the same appliqué.

In the example shown there will be just one appliqué base.

Fusible web paper–side up

Cut out the appliqué base shape from the fusible web about ¼" beyond the traced line.

Following the manufacturer's instructions, fuse the appliqué base shape to the wrong side of the black fabric.

Be certain the wrong side of the fabric is facing up and the paper side of the fusible is facing up so that the glue is in contact with the wrong side of the fabric.

Cut out the base carefully on the traced line.

Lay another piece of fusible web with the paper-side up over the pattern. For the colored pieces of each appliqué, trace around each individual shape of the design on the **INSIDE** edge of the heavy black outline. The green line on the diagram shows an example of where you will trace.

Cut out the appliqué shapes from the fusible web about ¼" beyond the traced lines.

You will save fabric if you trace shapes that will be ironed to the same color fabric close to each other on the fusible web. Be sure to leave about ½" of space between them.

You can easily keep track of what you have traced by giving each traced shape the same number you gave that area of the pattern. Check off each piece on the pattern as you trace it. When all the pieces are checked you are finished tracing.

Some appliqué shapes, such as the ladybug in the example, will require that you cut out pieces within the shape.

Draw an X through the shapes that need to be cut out of the interior of an appliqué shape.

Fuse the traced shapes to the wrong side of the fabrics you have chosen.

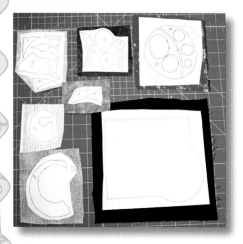

Carefully cut out each piece for your appliqués on the traced line.

Keep all the pieces in a tray, box, or basket until you have completed your appliqués.

Leave the paper backing on the black appliqué base. Turn the base so that the right side of the fabric is facing up.

Peel the paper backing from each colored piece and position it on the black appliqué base, leaving space between the colored pieces to form the black outlines.

Refer to the project photo to be certain colored pieces are correctly placed.

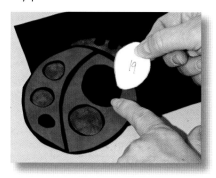

Fuse the colored sections in place following the manufacturer's instructions.

Peel the paper backing from the black appliqué base.

Position the completed appliqués on your project. Refer to the project photo for placement. Fuse in place.

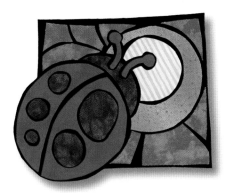

BASIC BORDER DIRECTIONS

Quilt borders seem so simple. After all, they are just long straight pieces of fabric. The problem lies in how you attach those borders to your quilt. Every quilter sews a little differently. Each time you cut a piece of fabric or sew a seam in your quilt, it is easy to be off by a fraction of an inch. Over an entire quilt top, those fractions add up. Your finished top may be smaller or larger than the top made by the pattern's creator. And that's okay as long as you measure and cut the border pieces in just the right way.

- First, measure your own quilt to determine the length to cut for the borders.

- Second, pin those border pieces to the quilt before sewing them on.

We use two basic types of borders in this book—borders with and without cornerstones. The measuring procedure is a little different for each type. Check the directions for the design you have chosen. Some designs have borders on all four sides and some do not. Be certain to check the cutting width for all borders on each quilt. Most of our designs have borders with different widths. The directions for your design will tell you how many pieces to cut for each border.

Measuring for a Border without Cornerstones

For this example the quilt has equal width borders on all four sides.

1. Measure the length of the quilt through the center from top to bottom.

   Cut 2 pieces to this length and the border width listed in the pattern for the side border pieces.

2. Fold the quilt and the side border pieces to find the center of each. Mark the centers with a pin.

   Use a pin to mark halfway between the centers and each end of the quilt and the side border pieces.

   Pin a side border piece to the left and right sides of the quilt. Match the pins together.

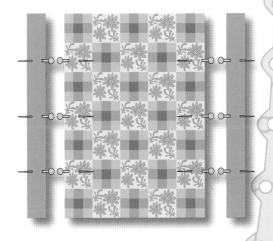

3. Without stretching the quilt or the border piece, sew the side border pieces to the left and right sides of the quilt.

   Press the seam toward the borders.

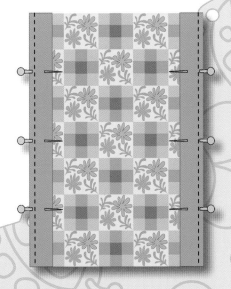

4. Measure the width of the quilt through the center from side to side including the side borders.

Cut 2 pieces to this measurement and the border width listed in the pattern for the top and bottom border pieces.

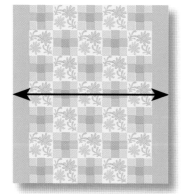

5. Fold, mark, pin, and sew the top and bottom borders in the same way you added the side borders.

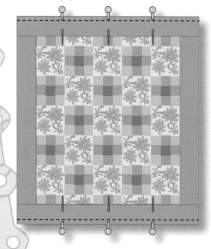

Measuring for a Border with Cornerstones

When your border includes cornerstones, measure both the length and width of the quilt before sewing any of the border pieces to the quilt.

For this example the quilt has equal width borders on all four sides.

1. Measure the length of the quilt through the center from top to bottom.

   Cut 2 pieces to this length and the border width listed in the pattern for the side border pieces.

2. Measure the width of the quilt through the center from side to side.

   Cut 2 pieces to this measurement and the border width listed in the pattern for the top and bottom border pieces.

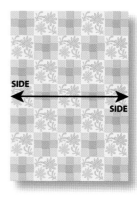

3. Fold the quilt and the side border pieces to find the center of each. Mark the centers with a pin.

   Use a pin to mark halfway between the centers and each end of the quilt and the border pieces.

   Pin a side border piece to the left and right sides of the quilt. Match the pins together.

4. Without stretching the quilt or the border piece, sew the side border pieces to the left and right sides of the quilt.

   Press the seams toward the borders.

5. Cut the cornerstones the size specified in the pattern.

6. Sew a cornerstone to each end of the top and bottom border pieces. Press the seams toward the border. Mark with pins as above and pin to the top and bottom of the quilt. Match the seams of the cornerstones and side border pieces.

7. Without stretching the quilt or the border piece, sew the top and bottom borders to the top and bottom of the quilt.

Press the seams toward the borders.

BINDINGS

See www.quiltedfrog.com/freetutorials/ for a video demonstration.

Your quilt is not complete until you have added an attractive binding to the edge. The binding acts as a frame for your quilt. This final step in the quiltmaking process can help to make your creation extra special. When choosing a fabric for the binding, choose a color or print that will provide a definite boundary to the quilt. A dark color is a good choice for binding. We love to use stripes and checks to add a whimsical touch that complements the colors and designs of our quilts. Pick the fabric that adds a perfect finish to your interpretation of our designs.

For all but two of the designs in this book we used a straight-cut binding. You can use either a straight-cut or bias-cut binding on any quilt that has straight edges. Designs with curved edges require a bias-cut binding.

Please note that you will need more fabric for a bias-cut binding. We give fabric requirements for straight-cut bindings for all designs except the Lady-Bug Apron and Monster Tic-Tac-Toe pieces, which have curved edges. If you choose to use a bias-cut binding on any of the other projects, you will need to check basic quilting books or the Internet to determine how much fabric to buy.

We prefer mitered bindings, which have a neater and more professional look that enhances the completed quilt. After all the work you put into the piecing and appliqué, your quilt deserves the very best binding.

Follow our step-by-step instructions to make a beautiful mitered binding (www.quiltedfrog.com/freetutorials/).

Read all the directions before starting.

Straight-Cut Mitered Binding

1. After quilting, trim the batting and backing even with the quilt top.

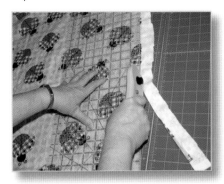

2. Cut the binding strips. We use 2½" wide strips.

The instructions for each design tell how many binding strips to cut. The quilt in this example requires 4 strips.

Trim the selvages from all the strips.

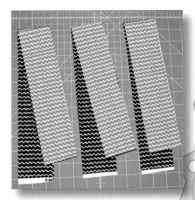

3. Set aside the first binding strip. Place the remaining strips on an ironing surface wrong-side up.

Fold the top right corner of each strip down to the lower edge of the strip. Press. We will call this the angled end of the strip.

4. Place the strip you set aside on your table with the right side of the fabric facing up.

With the wrong side facing up, place the angled end of a second strip on top of the end of the first strip. The overlapping strips will look like a backwards letter L. Pin the strips together along the fold.

Continue to pin all binding strips together in this way.

5. Stitch the strips together along the fold lines.

6. Trim the seam allowances to ¼".

7. Press the seams open.

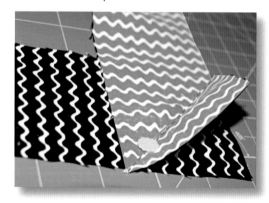

8. Fold the strips in half lengthwise, wrong-sides together, and press.

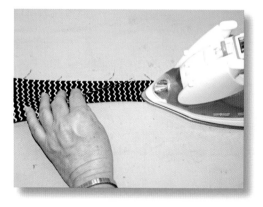

9. Starting in the center of one side of the quilt, lay the binding strip on the quilt with the raw edges even with the edge of the quilt.

Use a ¼" seam and begin sewing the binding to the quilt 8"–10" away from the end of the binding strip.

10. **Stop sewing ¼" from the corner.** With the needle in the fabric, turn the quilt and stitch out to the point of the corner at a 45-degree angle. Remove the quilt from the sewing machine. Trim the threads.

11. Fold the binding strip up at a right angle to the seam you just sewed.

You can see that as you make this fold you form the miter for the corner.

12. Fold the binding strip back down while holding the fold you just made. Keep the edge of the binding even with the edge of the quilt.

13. Starting at the very edge of the corner, sew the binding to the next side of the quilt. Keep the edge of the binding even with the edge of the quilt.

In the same way, sew around the remaining 3 corners. Stop sewing 8"–10" from where you started.

14. On the end of the binding strip to your right, place a pin to mark where it meets the left end.

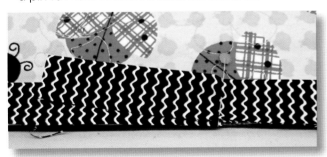

15. Trim this end of the binding 2½" away from the pin.

2½" is the width we cut straight-cut the binding strips for the projects in this book.

If you choose to make your binding strips a different width, make this cut the same as the width you originally cut your binding strips.

16. Fold the strip back on itself. Be certain to avoid twisting the strip.

17. Fold open the end you just cut so that the wrong side is facing up.

18. Fold the top right corner of the strip down to the lower edge as shown. Press. We call this the angled end of the strip.

19. Without twisting the strip, fold the left end of the binding open so that the right side of the fabric is facing up.

20. Place the angled end of the right hand binding strip over the non-angled end of the left hand binding strip. The overlapping strips will look like a backwards letter L. Pin the strips together along the pressed fold.

Fold the binding back to make certain it is not twisted.

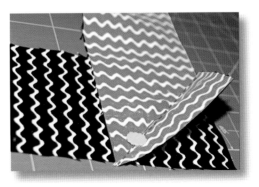

21. Stitch the strips together along the fold line marked in the photo for Step 20. Trim and press as before.

22. Trim the seam allowance to ¼" and press open.

23. Fold the joined binding strip and place the raw edges of the binding even with the edge of the quilt.

24. Check to be sure the binding is not twisted. Finish sewing the binding to the fourth side of the quilt.

25. On the front side of the quilt, fold the binding back over the seam and press.

Carefully press the corners into miters.

26. Press the binding over to the back of the quilt. Maintain the miter at the corners as you press.

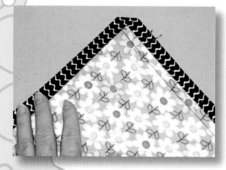

27. On the right side of the quilt, stitch in the ditch between the quilt and the binding to securely attach the binding to the back of the quilt and cover the seam.

Continuous Bias Binding

You need bias-cut binding to bind the curved edges of the LadyBug Apron and Monster Tic-Tac-Toe projects.

The diagrams are shown with solid color fabric to make it easier to understand the process. The green represents the right side of the fabric and yellow represents the wrong side of the fabric.

Cut a square the size called for in the pattern. Mark 2 opposite sides with pins.

Cut in half diagonally to make 2 triangles as shown.

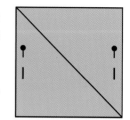

Place the pin-marked edges of the triangles right sides together and join with a ¼" seam. Press the seam open.

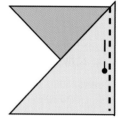

On the wrong side, draw lines parallel to the long edges, the distance between the lines equal to the desired width of the binding strips.

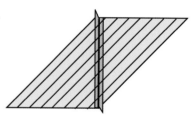

Bring the short edges together to form a tube with the right sides of the fabric to the inside. Align the raw edges, offsetting by the width of the binding strip so the lines match perfectly. Pin where drawn lines intersect.

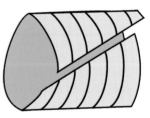

Sew the pinned edges together with a ¼" seam. Press the seam open.

At either side of the tube, start cutting directly on the drawn line. Continue cutting around the tube until you have one long strip of bias binding.

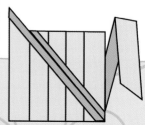

Proceed as with straight-cut binding.

PRINTING & ASSEMBLING THE APPLIQUÉ PATTERNS

See www.quiltedfrog.com/freetutorials/ for a video demonstration.

Appliqué Patterns

There are two different ways to print the patterns on 8½" x 11" paper. You just have to follow a few easy steps to make certain that your patterns will be the full size when printed.

Some of the patterns fit on one page and are printed with no scaling. These patterns will include the number "100" at the end of the file name. Most of the patterns print on several pages and must be printed so that part of the pattern on each page fits within the print margins of your printer. These patterns will include the word "FIT" at the end of the file name. We have sized the patterns so that they will align perfectly when you tape them together.

The directions for each pattern and the file name will tell you which method to use.

**Be sure to print on only one side of the paper.

Printing with No Page Scaling

If your pattern name include the number "100," the directions for that pattern will include a message like this at the beginning of the instructions:

PREPARE THE APPLIQUÉ PATTERN by printing pillowcase_100.pdf from the ladybugpatterns folder on the CD.

When you print the pattern, select None from the Page Scaling drop down menu.

Open the pattern file in Adobe Reader software. If the Adobe Reader program is not already on your computer, you can download it from the Download Reader file on the CD or free of charge at:

http://get.adobe.com/reader/?promoid=BUIGO

You can also install Adobe Reader from the CD. With the pattern file open in Adobe Reader, choose Print from the File menu.

You will see a print dialog box similar to the one below.

Click on the Page Scaling drop down menu and choose None.

Click on the Print button in the bottom right corner of the dialog box to print your pattern.

All the pattern pieces you need for your project will print full size on one page. Remember that all of the appliqué patterns are printed in reverse so that they will be correctly oriented when you have finished making the appliqués.

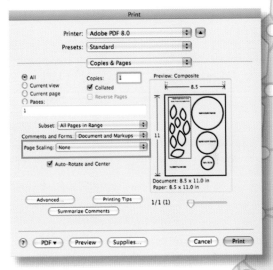

Printing Patterns That Fit to the Printer's Page Margins

If your pattern must be printed to fit the printer's page margins, the file name for that pattern will include the word "FIT."

The directions for that pattern will include a message like this at the beginning of the instructions:

PREPARE THE APPLIQUÉ PATTERN by printing quilt_fit.pdf from the ladybugpatterns folder on the CD.

Select Fit to Printable Area from the Page Scaling drop down menu.

With the pattern file open in Adobe Reader choose Print from the File menu.

You will see a print dialog box similar to the one shown on page 22.

Click on the Page Scaling drop down menu and choose Fit to Printable Area.

Click on the Print button in the bottom right corner of the dialog box to print your pattern.

The pattern pieces you need for your project will print full size on several pages. Remember that all of the appliqué patterns are printed in reverse so that they will be correctly oriented when you have finished making the appliqués.

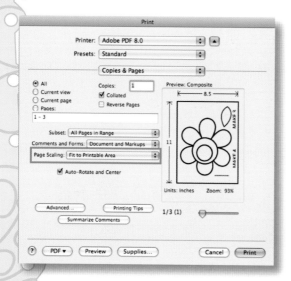

Each page of the pattern will have a large gray number.

Each pattern will include a diagram showing how to arrange the pages before you tape them together. The diagram will be similar to the one below.

The appliqués for the pattern in this example will print on two pages that should be arranged as shown.

Taping the Pattern Pages Together

After printing the pages for your pattern, look at the diagram in your pattern to see how to tape them together.

We will use the LEAP FROG PILLOWCASE pattern as the example in these instructions.

The LEAP FROG PILLOWCASE pattern prints on two pages that look like this.

Turn the pages horizontally and trim the margin from the edges of the page that will overlap another page of the pattern.

In this example the right edge of page 1 needs to be trimmed. Tape the edges together.

Overlap page 1 on page 2. Position page 1 so that all of the lines meet the lines on page 2.

Tape the overlapping edges of the pages together and you are ready to start making your appliqués.

Additional files are provided so that you can take the CD to a print shop, or architectural blueprint or office supply store, and have the patterns printed on a single sheet each. Be sure to check patterns for accuracy before using them.

Large format file names all end with _lf.pdf and are in the Large Format folder on the CD or you can click on the factory icon ▐ on the pattern index.

Lovely LadyBugs

*Bright Version of the L*ADY*B*UG Q*UILT• Finished size 46" x 61"*

LadyBug Quilt

Strips are cut selvage to selvage.
Use ¼" seam allowance.

MATERIALS	BRIGHT VERSION	TRADITIONAL VERSION
Block 1	1 Yard Green Solid	1 Yard Pink Solid
Block 2 & Cornerstones	⅝ Yard Green Print FABRIC A ⅝ Yard Orange FABRIC B	⅝ Yard Green Print FABRIC A ⅝ Yard Orange FABRIC B
Block 2 Centers & Cornerstones	¼ Yard Pink FABRIC C	¼ Yard Dark Red FABRIC C
Appliqué Bases	1 Yard Solid Black	1 Yard Solid Black
Paper-Backed Fusible Web	4 Yards	4 Yards
LadyBug Bodies & Antennae	Fat Quarter Dark Pink	Fat Quarter Dark Red
LadyBug Spots & Heads	Fat Quarter Navy Blue	Fat Quarter Brown
Flower Petals	⅜ Yard Medium Blue	⅜ Yard Medium Teal
Outer Flower Centers	Fat Quarter Dark Blue	Fat Quarter Light Teal
Inner Flower Centers	8" x 11" Yellow	8" x 11" Gold
Leaves	Fat Quarter Green	Fat Quarter Green
Stems	2 pkgs. Green Jumbo Rickrack (5 Yards ⅝" wide)	2 pkgs. Green Jumbo Rickrack (5 Yards ⅝" wide)
Borders 1 & 3 and Binding	¾ Yard Black & White Stripe	¾ Yard Pink Stripe
Border 2	⅜ Yard Pink	⅜ Yard Pink
Border 4	⅞ Yard Green Print	⅞ Yard Green Print
Batting	1½ Yards 96" wide	1½ Yards 96" wide
Backing	3 Yards Pink Print	3 Yards Brown Print

Traditional Version of the LadyBug Quilt

PREPARE THE APPLIQUÉ PATTERN by printing 01lb_quilt_fit.pdf from the ladybugpatterns folder on the CD.

Select Fit to Printable Area from the Page Scaling drop down menu. (See detailed printing instructions, pages 21–22.)

Tape the pages together according to the diagram. Trim the excess white border from adjoining pages as necessary.

| 1 | 2 | 3 | 4 |

Directions are for the bright version of the quilt. Use the photo and the materials list to substitute the fabric colors if you are making the traditional version of the quilt.

Please note that all 4 cornerstones of the traditional version are cut from the same fabric rather than 2 fabrics as in the bright version.

Block 1

Cut 4 strips 6½" wide of solid green.

Cut 24 blocks 6½" x 6½" from the strips.

Make 24 blocks

Block 2–Nine-Patch

Cut 7 strips 2½" wide of green print (FABRIC A).

Cut 6 strips 2½" wide of orange (FABRIC B).

Cut 2 strips 2½" wide of pink (FABRIC C).

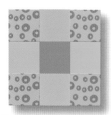

Make 24 Nine-Patch blocks.

Sew the Blocks Together

Sew the blocks together as shown to make 8 rows of 5 blocks each.

Sew the 8 rows together so that your quilt top has a checkerboard appearance.

Make 4 rows like this.

Make 4 rows like this.

Make the Borders

Measure both the length and width of the quilt top before cutting the borders.

Border 1

Cut 9 strips 1" wide of black & white stripe and join them end-to-end.

Add Border 1 to all 4 sides of the quilt. (See detailed Border instructions on page 15.)

Save the remaining strip for Border 3.

Border 2

Cut 5 strips 2½" wide of pink and join them end-to-end.

Add Border 2 to all 4 sides of the quilt.

Border 3

Use the remaining black & white fabric strip and add Border 3 to all 4 sides of the quilt.

Border 4

Measure the length and width of the quilt including Border 3 before adding Border 4. Record these measurements.
Length= _____
Width = _____
All border 4 strips are cut from the green print.

Cut 2 strips 1½" wide and join end-to-end. Cut to the length measurement recorded above and add to the right side of the quilt.

Cut 2 strips 3½" wide and join end-to-end. Cut to the length measurement recorded above and add to the left side of the quilt.

Cut the cornerstones as follows:
Upper left cornerstone:
Cut 1 dark pink 3½" x 4½" rectangle.
Upper right cornerstone:
Cut 1 orange 1½" x 4½" rectangle.
Lower left cornerstone:
Cut 1 orange 3½" x 3½" square.
Lower right cornerstone:
Cut 1 dark pink 1½" x 3½" rectangle.

Cut 2 strips 4½" wide and join end-to-end. Cut to the width measurement recorded above and add the cornerstones as shown (page 27). Add to the top of the quilt.

Cut 2 strips 3½" wide. Cut to the width measurement recorded above and add the cornerstones as shown.

Add to the bottom of the quilt.

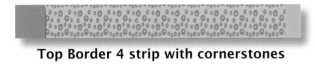

Top Border 4 strip with cornerstones

Bottom Border 4 strip with cornerstones

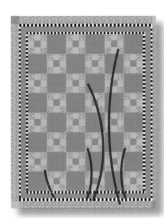

Sew the rickrack stem in place. Use the dotted lines on the appliqué pattern as a guide.

Appliqués

Make all appliqués for the quilt. (Refer to the Easy Out-Line Appliqué Technique, pages 12–14.)

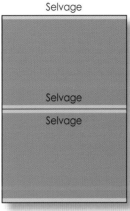

The 23 appliqué bases look like this.

After making all the appliqués remove the paper backing from the fusible. Fuse in place following the manufacturer's instructions. Refer to the photo for placement.

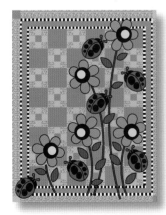

The LadyBug quilting design is available from www. quiltedfrog.com/shop/category/machine-quilting-designs-by-quilted-frog/

Finishing the Quilt

Cut the backing fabric into two 1½ yard lengths.

Sew together along the selvages with a 1½" seam.

Trim the selvages off, leaving a ¼" seam allowance. Press open.

Selvage

Selvage

Selvage

Selvage

Layer the quilt, batting, and backing. The batting and backing should be 2"–4" bigger than the quilt on all 4 sides.

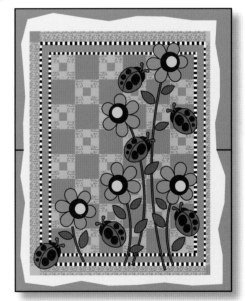

Quilt by hand or machine. Trim the batting and backing even with the quilt top.

Cut 6 strips 2½" wide of black for the binding and join end-to-end.

Press the binding strip in half lengthwise. Use this binding strip and your favorite method to bind the quilt. We prefer a mitered binding (page 17).

**Basic
Pillowcase
Pattern**
(page 8)

**Easy OutLine
Appliqué
Technique**
(page 12)

Read all instructions
before starting.

This pillowcase is a little different.
Cuff A is pieced

Strips are cut selvage to selvage unless otherwise noted.
Use ¼" seam allowance.

MATERIALS

Cuff A Sky	¼ Yard Orange Print
Cuff A Ground, Cuff B & Cuff C	⅞ Yard Light Green Print
Border	⅛ Yard Black & White Stripe
Pillowcase Body	⅔ Yard Bright Pink Print or Solid Fabric
LadyBug Body & Antennae	8" x 8" Dark Pink
LadyBug Spots & Head	7" x 7" Navy Blue
Flower Petals	12" x 10" Medium Blue
Outer Flower Centers	6" x 6" Dark Blue
Inner Flower Centers	5" x 5" Yellow
Leaves	6" x 6" Green
Stems	½ Yard Green Mini-Rickrack
Appliqué Bases	Fat Quarter Solid Black
Lightweight Batting	26" x 16"
Paper-Backed Fusible Web	½ Yard

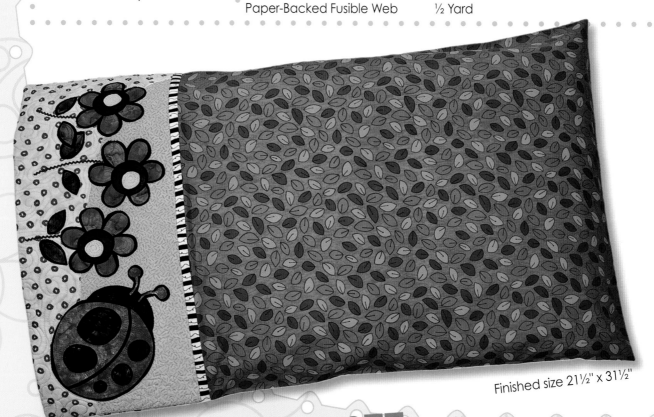

Finished size 21½" x 31½"

LadyBug Pillowcase

PREPARE THE APPLIQUÉ PATTERN AND CUFF by printing 02lb_case_fit.pdf

and

03lb_cuff_fit.pdf from the ladybugpatterns folder on the CD.

Select Fit to Printable Area from the Page Scaling drop down menu. (See detailed printing instructions, pages 21–22.)

Tape the pages together according to the diagrams. Trim the excess white border from adjoining pages as necessary.

APPLIQUÉ PATTERN

| 1 | 2 |

CUFF PATTERN

1	2
3	4
5	6

Appliqués

Make all appliqués for the pillowcase. (Refer to the Easy OutLine Appliqué Technique, pages 12–14.)

Appliqué patterns are printed in mirror image so they will be the same direction as the photo when the pillowcase is complete.

After making all the appliqués remove the paper backing from the fusible.

The 9 appliqué bases look like this.

Pillowcase Cuff

Fabric widths can vary from 40"–44" wide. Make certain you use no more than half the fabric width for Cuff A and Cuff B.

The Cuff A section is pieced before fusing the appliqués to it. The pattern pieces are a little larger than the finished Cuff A measurements to allow for take-up while quilting. It is trimmed to the correct size after quilting.

Cut 1 Cuff A—Sky of orange print fabric.
Cut 1 Cuff A—Ground of green print fabric.

With right sides together, match the notches and sew together with a ¼" seam. The seam line is marked on the pattern pieces with a dotted line. Press the seam toward the green fabric.

Sew rickrack stems in place before adding the appliqués. The stem placement is marked on the appliqué pattern with a dotted line.

Place all of the appliqués on Cuff A. Use the original pattern and picture of the finished pillowcase as placement guides. Fuse the appliqués in place following the fusible manufacturer's instructions.

Layer the batting with Cuff A, with the fused appliqués right-side up. Pin or baste the 2 layers together and quilt by machine. Trim the quilted cuff to measure 21½" x 9".

Cut 1 strip 21½" x 9" of light green for Cuff B. Cut 1 strip 43" x 9" of light green for Cuff C.

Finish the cuff according to the Basic Pillowcase instructions (pages 8–11).

Pillowcase Body

Square up the cut edges of the ⅔ yard pillowcase body fabric.

Cut a border strip 1¼" wide of black & white fabric. Sew to the top edge of the body.

Cut off the selvages and trim the body and cuff to the same width.

Fold the body in half, aligning the selvage-trimmed edges, right sides together. Sew the long sides and the end opposite the border strip. Turn the body right-side out. Press flat.

Complete the Cuff

Join the short ends of the cuff unit and press the seam open.

Fold the cuff in half along the long seam, wrong sides together with the appliqué facing out.

Baste the raw edges together by machine or hand.

Sew Cuff to Body

Join the cuff to the border on the body according to the instructions on page 11.

Turn the cuff right-side out and press the seam flat.

Your pillowcase is complete and ready to use.

Variations

Reverse the appliqué patterns and position of the appliqués.

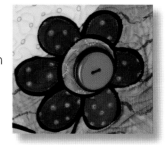

Stack a 1⅝" and 1¼" button and sew to the center of each of the flowers.

Piece various widths of fabric strips for the pillowcase body. Include a checkerboard strip just for fun.

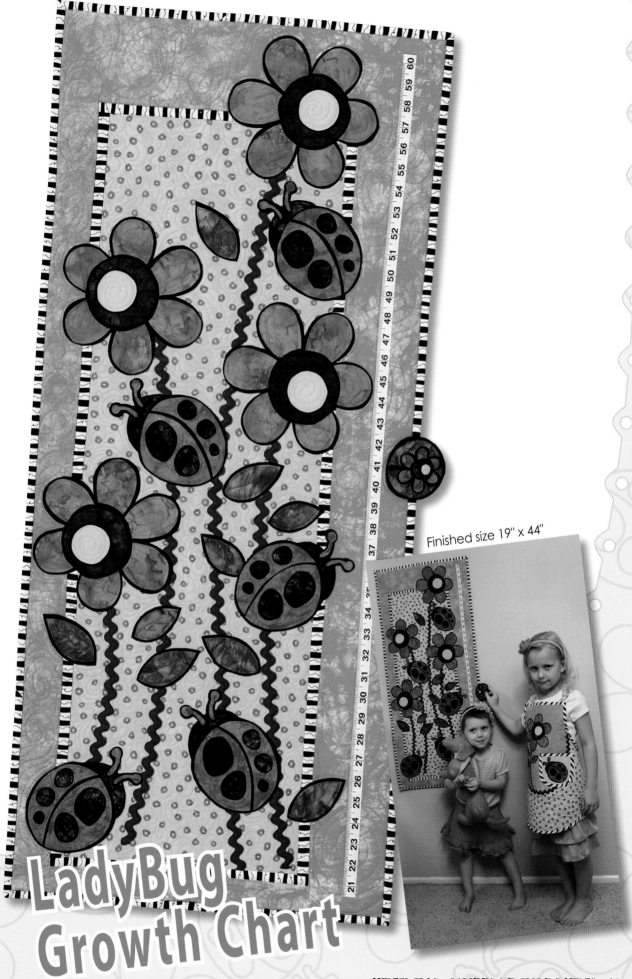

LadyBug
Growth Chart

Finished size 19" x 44"

REFERENCE INSTRUCTIONS

Basic Border Directions
(page 15)

Easy OutLine Appliqué Technique
(page 12)

Mitered Binding Directions
(page 17)

Read all instructions before starting.

MATERIALS

Quilt Center	⅜ Yard Green Print
Border 1 & Binding	½ Yard Black & White Stripe
Border 2	½ Yard Pink
LadyBug Bodies & Antennae	Fat Quarter Dark Pink
LadyBug Spots & Heads	Fat Quarter Navy Blue
Flower Petals	⅓ Yard Medium Blue
Large Flower Centers	Fat Quarter Dark Blue
Small Flower Centers	8" x 11" Yellow
Leaves	11" x 11" Green
Stems	2 packages Green Jumbo Rickrack (5 yards ⅝" wide
Appliqué Bases	⅔ Yard Solid Black
Paper-Backed Fusible Web	3½ Yards
Backing	1½ Yards Pink Print
Batting	⅔ Yard
Additional Supplies	60" Measuring Tape

PREPARE THE APPLIQUÉ PATTERN by printing 04lb_growth_fit.pdf from the ladybugpatterns folder on the CD.

Select Fit to Printable Area from the Page Scaling drop down menu. (See detailed printing instructions, pages 21–22.)

Tape the pages together according to the diagram. Trim the excess white border from adjoining pages as necessary.

Background

Cut 1 rectangle 12½" x 37½" of green print for the chart center.

Borders

Border 1
Cut 3 strips 1" wide of black & white stripe and join end-to-end.

Add Border 1 to all 4 sides of the chart. (See detailed Border instructions on page 15.)

Save the remaining strip for Border 3.

Border 2
From the pink, cut:
1 strip 4½" wide (right side)
1 strip 2½" wide (left side)
1 strip 5" wide (top)
1 strip 2" wide (bottom)

Measure, cut, and add each Border 2 strip to the chart as shown.

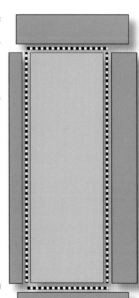

Rickrack Stems & Appliqués

Using the photo and the diagram as guides, sew the rickrack stems in place. Tuck under the ends that will not be covered by appliqués so they will not ravel.

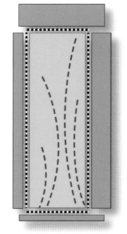

Make all appliqués for the growth chart. (Refer to the Easy OutLine Appliqué Terchnique, pages 12–14.)

The flower circle is for marking your child's height on the chart. You may want to make several.

Remember that all appliqué patterns are printed in mirror image so they will be the same direction as the photo when the chart is complete.

After making all the appliqués remove the paper backing from the fusible. Position on the chart and fuse in place following the manufacturer's instructions. Use the photo and figure as placement guides.

Make 4   Make 3   Make 6   Make 3   Make 2

Make as many as you will need

The 19 appliqué bases look like this.

Finishing the Growth Chart

Quilting
Layer the chart, batting, and backing. The batting and backing should be several inches bigger than the chart on all 4 sides.

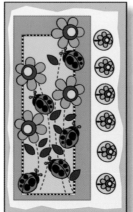

Quilt by hand or machine. Trim the batting and backing even with growth chart.

Binding
Cut 4 strips 2½" wide of the black & white stripe and join end-to-end.

Press the binding strip in half lengthwise. Use this binding strip and your favorite method to bind the chart. We prefer a mitered binding (page 17).

Cut off the first 21½" of the tape measure.

Position the tape measure on the chart and use pins to hold it in place as shown. You do not want to put the pins through the tape measure because the holes will be permanent.

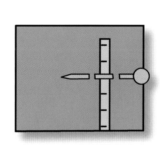

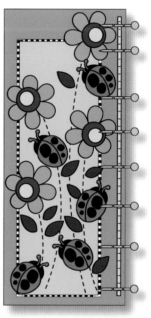

Sew the tape measure in place along both sides with a machine basting stitch.

Using the Growth Chart

Hang the growth chart so that the 21½" mark on the tape measure is 21½" from the floor.

Mark your child's height with a pin.

Write your child's name and the date on one of the markers. Sew the marker to the chart with the stem of the flower touching the appropriate spot on the tape measure.

Finished size 15½" x 13½"

LadyBug Apron

Strips are cut selvage to selvage.
Use ¼" seam allowance.

MATERIALS

Apron Body	¾ Yard Pink
Apron Facing	Fat Quarter Green Print
Pocket	14" x 7" Light Orange
LadyBug Body & Antennae	7" x 12" Dark Pink
LadyBug Spots & Head	7" x 8" Navy Blue
Flower Petals	Fat Quarter Medium Blue
Large Flower Center	4" x 12" Dark Blue
Small Flower Center	8" x 4" Yellow
Leaves	5" x 8" Green
Stems	8" Green Medium Rickrack
Apron Trim	1 Yard Green Jumbo Rickrack
Appliqué Base	9" x 11" Solid Black
Paper-Backed Fusible Web	½ Yard
Backing	1 Yard Pink Print
Batting	1 Yard 44" Wide Prewashed Flannel
Binding	Fat Quarter Black & White Stripe

REFERENCE INSTRUCTIONS

Easy OutLine Appliqué Technique
(page 12)

Continuous Bias Binding Directions
(page 20)

Read all instructions before starting.

PREPARE THE APPLIQUÉ and APRON PATTERNS by printing 05lb_apron_fit.pdf, selecting Fit to Printable Area from the Page Scaling drop down menu,

and

06lb_aprnapp_100.pdf, selecting None from the Page Scaling drop down menu. (See detailed printing instructions, pages 21–22.) Both patterns are in the ladybugpatterns folder on the CD.

Tape the apron pattern pages together according to the diagram. Trim the excess white border from adjoining pages as necessary.

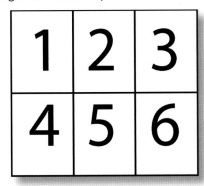

Appliqués

Make all appliqués for the apron. (Refer to the Easy OutLine Appliqué Techinque, pages 12–14.)

After making all the appliqués remove the paper backing from the fusible.

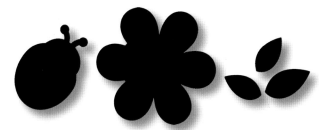

The 5 appliqué bases look like this.

Apron Body

Fold the pink in half, right-side out, and cut out the Apron Body, placing one edge against the fold as shown.

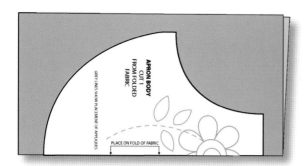

Using the photo and the diagram as guides, sew the medium rickrack stem in place. The ends will be covered by the appliqué and the apron facing.

Layer the apron top, batting, and backing.

Position and fuse the flower and leaf appliqués onto the apron following the manufacturer's instructions. Be certain the flower appliqué covers the raw end of the rickrack.

Quilt by hand or machine.

Trim the batting and backing even with the apron top.

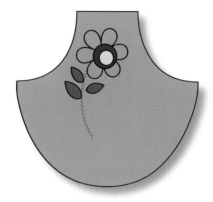

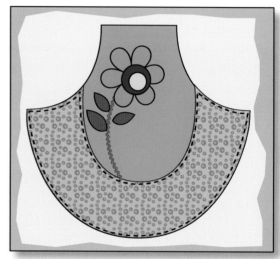

Fold the green print in half, right-side out, and cut out the Apron Facing, placing one edge against the fold as shown.

Sew the jumbo rickrack over the raw upper edge of the facing.

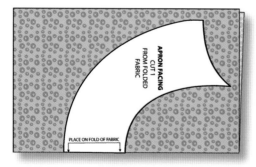

Place the green facing right-side up on the right side of the pink apron. Pin the facing in place and sew around all 4 sides ¼" from the edge. Be certain the facing covers the raw end of the rickrack.

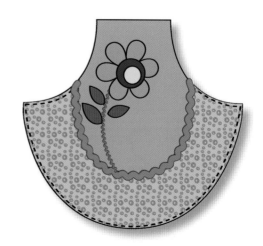

Pocket

Fold the 14" x 7" rectangle of orange in half. Press a crease along the fold.

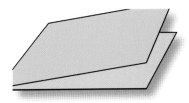

Unfold and trace the pocket shape onto the right side as shown.

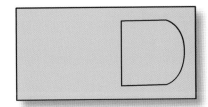

Fuse the ladybug appliqué in place inside the traced pocket outline.

Cut 1 square 7" x 7" of flannel. Fold the pocket in half again with the flannel inside the fold.

Quilt the pocket.

Trim the quilted pocket along the traced outline.

Binding

Cut an 18" x 18" square of black & white stripe to make continuous bias binding (page 20).

Finishing the Apron

Straps & Loops

Cut 2 strips 3" x 36½" of green print for the straps.

Fold in half lengthwise, right sides together. Sew down the long side and across one end for each strap. Turn the straps right-side out and press flat.

Cut 2 rectangles 2" x 4" from the black & white bias strip for the loops.

Press under ¼" on both of the long sides, then fold in half wrong sides together. Top stitch close to the open side.

Stitch the straps and loops in place as shown.

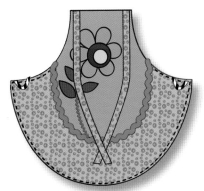

Binding the Apron & Pocket

Cut an 18" x 18" square of black & white stripe to make continuous 2½" wide bias binding. Press the long bias strip in half lengthwise. Be careful not to stretch the strip while you are pressing.

Use this binding strip and your favorite method to bind the apron and pocket. We prefer a mitered binding (page 17).

Stitch the pocket in place on the apron.

Finished size 9" x 18"

LadyBug Chair Back Covers

REFERENCE INSTRUCTIONS

Easy OutLine Appliqué Technique
(page 12)

Mitered Binding Instructions
(page 17)

Read all instructions before starting.

MATERIALS FOR 2

Background	⅓ Yard Light Green
Sashes	1 Yard Pink
LadyBug Body & Antennae	7" x 12" Dark Pink
LadyBug Spots & Head	7" x 8" Navy Blue
Flower Petals	6" x 6" Medium Blue
Outer Flower Center	5" x 10" Dark Blue
Inner Flower Center	6" x 3" Yellow
Leaves	4" x 6" Green
Appliqué Base	16" x 8" Solid Black Fabric
Paper-Backed Fusible Web	1 Yard
Backing	½ Yard Pink Print
Batting	½ Yard 44" Wide
Binding	¼ Yard Black & White Stripe

PREPARE THE APPLIQUÉ PATTERN by printing 07lb_chair_100.pdf from the ladybugpatterns folder on the CD.

Select None from the Page Scaling drop down menu. (See detailed printing instructions, pages 21–22.)

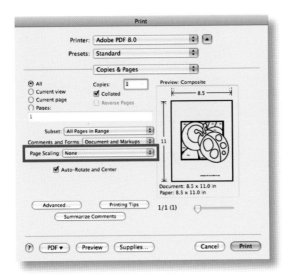

Chair Covers

Cut 2 rectangles 9" x 18" of light green for the background.

Appliqués

Make all appliqués for the chair back covers. (Refer to the **Easy OutLine Appliqué** Technique, pages 12–14.)

Remember that all appliqué patterns are printed in mirror image so they will be the same direction as the photo when the covers are complete.

After making all the appliqués remove the paper backing from the fusible.

The appliqué base looks like this. Make 2.

Position the appliqués and fuse in place following the manufacturer's instructions. Refer to the chair back cover photo and figure for placement.

Right Side of Fabric

Finishing the Chair Back Covers

Quilting

Layer the chair back covers with the batting and backing. Quilt by hand or machine. Trim the batting and backing even with the chair cover top.

Sashes

Cut 4 strips 8½" x 36" of pink for the sashes.

Fold each strip in half lengthwise, right sides together. Sew one short end and the long side together. Turn right-side out. Press flat.

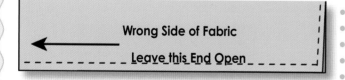

Wrong Side of Fabric

Leave this End Open

Pin a finished sash to both sides of each chair back cover. The lower edge of the sash should be 2 ½" from the lower edge of the chair cover. Sew in place.

Binding

Cut 4 strips 2½" wide of black & white stripes and join end-to-end.

Press the binding strip in half lengthwise. Use this binding strip and your favorite method to bind the quilt. We prefer a mitered binding (page 17). Be careful to avoid catching the sashes in the seam as you apply the binding.

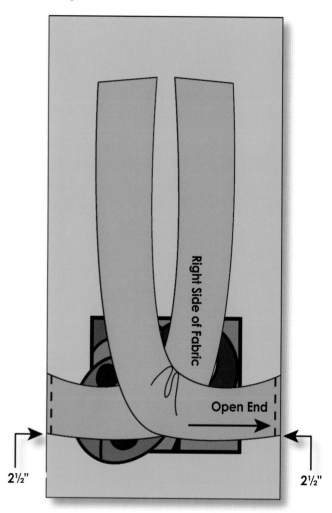

Right Side of Fabric

Open End

2½"   2½"

Finished size 14" x 15¾"

LadyBug Placemat

REFERENCE INSTRUCTIONS

Basic Border Directions
(page 15)

Easy OutLine Appliqué Technique
(page 12)

Mitered Binding Directions
(page 17)

Read all instructions before starting.

Strips are cut selvage to selvage.
Use ¼" seam allowance.

MATERIALS FOR 2 PLACEMATS

Placemat Center	⅓ Yard Orange
Sashes	1 Yard Pink
LadyBug Body & Antennae	7" x 12" Dark Pink
LadyBug Spots & Head	7" x 8" Navy Blue
Flower Petals	Fat Quarter Medium Blue
Outer Flower Center	4" x 12" Dark Blue
Inner Flower Center	8" x 4" Yellow
Leaves	5" x 8" Green
Appliqué Base	½ Yard Solid Black
Border 1 & Binding	½ Yard Black & White Stripe
Border 2	¼ yard Light Green Print
Paper-Backed Fusible Web	2 Yards
Batting	½ Yard 44" Wide
Backing	½ Yard Pink Print

PREPARE THE APPLIQUÉ PATTERN by printing 08lb_mat_fit.pdf from the ladybugpatterns folder on the CD.

Select Fit to Printable Area from the Page Scaling drop down menu. (See detailed printing instructions, pages 21–22.)

Tape the pages together according to the diagram. Trim the excess white border from adjoining pages as necessary.

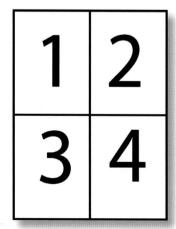

Placemat Backgrounds

Cut 2 squares 9½" x 9½" of orange for the placemat centers.

Borders

Border 1
All the Border 1 strips are cut from the black & white stripe.

Cut 2 strips 1" wide.

Cut 4 segments 9½" x 1" and add to the top and bottom of each placemat center.

Cut 4 segments 10½" x 1" and add to the sides.

Border 2
All the Border 2 strips are cut from the light green print.

Cut 2 strips 2¼" wide.

Cut 4 segments 10½" x 2¼" and sew to the top and bottom of each placemat.

Cut 2 segments 14" x 2¼" and sew to the right side of each placemat.

Cut 1 strip 4" wide.

Cut 2 segments 14½" x 4" and sew to the left side of each placemat.

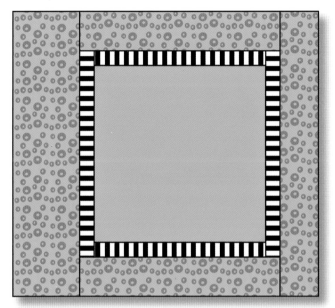

Appliqués

Make all appliqués for the placemats. (Refer to the Easy OutLine Appliqué Technique, pages 12–14.)

Remember that all appliqué patterns are printed in mirror image so they will be the same direction as the photo when the quilt is complete.

After making all the appliqués remove the paper backing from the fusible. Position and fuse in place following the manufacturer's instructions. Refer to the photo and diagram for placement.

The appliqué base looks like this. Make 2.

Finishing the Placemats

Quilting
Layer the placemats, batting, and backing. The batting and backing should be several inches bigger than the placemats on all 4 sides.

Quilt by hand or machine. Trim the batting and backing even with the placemat top.

Binding
Cut 4 strips 2 ½" wide of the black & white stripe and join end-to-end.

Press the binding strip in half lengthwise. Use this binding strip and your favorite method to bind the placemats. We prefer a mitered binding (page 17).

Cars, Cars, Cars

Finished size 44"x 62"

Car Quilt

REFERENCE INSTRUCTIONS

Basic Nine-Patch Quilt Pattern
(page 5)

Basic Border Directions
(page 15)

Easy OutLine Appliqué Technique
(page 12)

Mitered Binding Instructions
(page 17)

Read all instructions before starting.

MATERIALS	
Block 1 & Cornerstone	1 Yard Black Print
Block 2	½ Yard Medium Blue Print FABRIC A
	½ Yard Green Print FABRIC B
Block 2 Centers	⅓ Yard Red FABRIC C
Appliqué Bases	⅝ Yard Solid Black
Paper-Backed Fusible Web	2½ Yards
Cars	Fat Quarter Red
	Fat Quarter Blue
Wheels	⅛ Yard Gray
People Faces	6"x 6" Flesh
Trees	⅛ Yard Each Brown,
	Light Green, and Dark Green
Sun, Headlights	⅛ Yard Yellow
Mountains	12" x 6" Light Purple
	12" x 6" Dark Purple
Mountain Top & Inside Windows	⅛ Yard White
Borders 1 & 3	¼ Yard Black
Border 2	½ Yard Yellow Stripe
Border 4	⅔ Yard Light Blue
Binding	½ Yard Black
Batting	1½ Yards 96" wide
Backing	3 Yards Blue Print

PREPARE THE APPLIQUÉ PATTERN by printing 09car_quilt_fit.pdf from the ladybugpatterns folder on the CD.

Select Fit to Printable Area from the Page Scaling drop down menu. (See detailed printing instructions, pages 21–22.)

Tape the pages together according to the diagram. Trim the excess white border from adjoining pages as necessary.

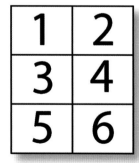

Block 1

Cut 4 strips 6½" wide of black print.

Cut 20 blocks 6½" x 6½" from the strips.

Cut 1 square 3" x 3" for the cornerstone in Border 2.

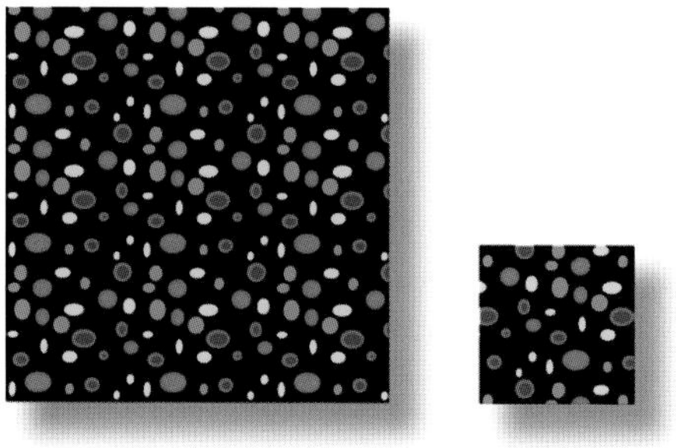

Block 2–Nine-Patch

Cut 5 strips 2½" wide of blue print (FABRIC A).

Cut 6 strips 2½" wide of green (FABRIC B).

Cut 2 strips 2½" wide of red (FABRIC C).

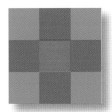

Make 20 Nine-Patch blocks.

Sew the Blocks Together

Sew the blocks together as shown to make 8 rows of 5 blocks each.

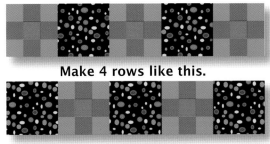

Make 4 rows like this.

Make 4 rows like this.

Sew the 8 rows together so that your quilt top has a checkerboard appearance.

Make the Borders

Border 1
Cut 6 strips 1" wide of black and join end-to-end.

Add Border 1 to all four sides of the quilt. (See detailed Border instructions on page 15.)

Save the remaining strip for Border 3.

Border 2
Cut 5 strips 3" wide of yellow stripe and join end-to-end.

Add Border 2 to the sides and bottom of the quilt.

Cut 3" off one end of the top border strip and add the cornerstone to the cut end. Add the top border with the cornerstone as shown.

Border 3
Use the remaining black fabric strip to cut and add Border 3 to the top and right side only.

Border 4
Cut 3 strips 7¼" wide of light blue and join end-to-end.

Add Border 4 to the top and right sides only. Make sure that the cornerstone is in the top right hand corner of the quilt as shown.

Appliqués

Make all appliqués for the quilt. (Refer to the Easy Out-Line Appliqué Technique, pages 12–14.)

Remember that all appliqué patterns are printed in mirror image so they will be the same direction as the photo when the quilt is complete.

After making all the appliqués remove the paper backing from the fusible. Fuse in place following the manufacturer's instructions. Refer to the photo for placement.

The 11 appliqué bases look like this.

Finishing the Quilt

Cut the backing fabric into two 1½ yard lengths.

Sew together along the selvages with a 1½" seam.

Trim the selvages off, leaving a ¼" seam allowance. Press open.

Layer the quilt, batting, and backing. The batting and backing should be several inches bigger than the quilt on all 4 sides.

Quilt by hand or machine. Trim the batting and backing even with quilt top.

Cut 6 strips 2½" wide of black for the binding and join end-to-end.

Press the binding strip in half lengthwise. Use this binding strip and your favorite method to bind the quilt. We prefer a mitered binding (page 17).

Quilting Suggestion

The Cars quilting design is available at our website, www.quiltedfrog.com/shop/category/quilting-designs-by-quilted-frog/

REFERENCE INSTRUCTIONS

Basic Pillowcase Pattern
(page 8)

Easy OutLine Appliqué Technique
(page 12)

Read all instructions before starting.

The cuff for this pillowcase is a little different from the basic pillowcase. Cuff A is pieced from two rectangles.

MATERIALS

Item	Material
Cuff A—Sky	¼ Yard Light Blue
Cuff A—Road, Cuff B, Cuff C	⅝ Yard Yellow Stripe
Border	⅛ Yard Red
Pillowcase Body	⅔ Yard Multicolor Print or Solid
Dog Body	8" x 11" Light Brown
Dog Face	4" x 5" Dark Brown
Dog Mouth	1" x 1" Dark Pink
Dog Tongue	2" x 2" Light Pink
Dog Nose & Eyebrows	4" x 4" Orange
Car, Ball, Dog Mouth	6" x 11" Red
Wheels	6" x 4" Grey
Trees	5" x 5" Light Green 5" x 5" Dark Green
Headlight	1½" x 1½" Yellow
Wheel Spokes, Ball, Car Handle	4" x 5" Turquoise
Headlight Rim, Windows, Dog Eyes	4" x 5" White
Driver's Face	2" x 2" Flesh
Appliqué Base	24" x 9" Solid Black
Lightweight Batting	26" x 14"
Paper-Backed Fusible Web	1 Yard

Finished size 21½" x 31½"

Car Pillowcase

PREPARE THE APPLIQUÉ PATTERN by printing 10car_case_fit.pdf from the ladybugpatterns folder on the CD.

Select Fit to Printable Area from the Page Scaling drop down menu. (See detailed printing instructions, pages 21–22.)

Tape the pages together according to the diagram at right. Trim the excess white border from adjoining pages as necessary.

Appliqués

Make all appliqués for the pillowcase. (Refer to the Easy OutLine Appliqué Technique, pages 12–14.)

One appliqué is the ball. The other appliqué includes the rest of the picture.

Remember that all appliqué patterns are printed in mirror image so they will be the same direction as the photo when the pillowcase is complete.

After making all the appliqués remove the paper backing from the fusible.

Base 1   Base 2
The 2 appliqué bases look like this.

Pillowcase Cuff

Fabric widths can vary from 40"–44" wide. Make certain you use no more than half the fabric width for Cuff A and Cuff B.

Make Cuff A
Cut 1 strip 22" x 6½" of light blue.
Cut 1 strip 22" x 4¼" of yellow stripe.
Place right sides together and sew the long sides together.

Press the seam toward the blue section.

Position the appliqués on Cuff A. Use the original pattern and picture of the finished pillowcase as placement guides. Make sure that the black horizon line of the appliqué aligns with the seam. Fuse the appliqués in place following the fusible manufacturer's instructions.

Layer the batting with Cuff A, with the fused appliqués right-side up. Pin or baste the 2 layers together and quilt by machine. Trim the quilted Cuff A to measure 21½" x 9½".

Cut 1 strip 21½" x 9 ½" of yellow stripe for Cuff B. Cut 1 strip 43" x 9½" of yellow stripe for Cuff C.

Finish the cuff according to the Basic Pllowcase instructions (pages 8–11).

Pillowcase Body

Square up the cut edges of the ⅔ yard pillowcase body fabric.

Cut 1 border strip 1¼" wide of red fabric. Sew to the top edge of the body.

Cut off the selvages and trim the body and cuff to the same width.

Fold the body in half, aligning the selvage-trimmed edges, right sides together. Sew the long sides and the end opposite the border with a ¼" seam. Turn the body right-side out. Press flat.

Complete the Cuff

Join the short ends of the cuff unit and press the seam open.

Fold the cuff in half along the long seam with the wrong sides of the fabric together and the appliqué facing out.

Baste the raw edges together by machine or hand.

Sew Cuff to Body

Join the cuff and the body according to the instructions on page 11.

Turn the cuff right-side out and press the seam flat.

Your pillowcase is complete and ready to use.

Finished size 20" x 42"

Nearly No Sew Car Growth Chart

REFERENCE INSTRUCTIONS

Easy OutLine Appliqué Technique
(page 12)

Mitered Binding Directions
(page 17)

Read all instructions before starting.

This pattern does not require any sewing to make the quilt top. The only stitching is the quilting.

Strips are cut selvage to selvage.
Use ¼" seam allowance.

MATERIALS

Background	⅝ Yard Dark Blue
Truck	Fat Quarter Red
Car	Fat Quarter Blue
Wheels	12" x 12" Grey
Trees	Fat Quarter Each Light Green and Dark Green
Road	¼ Yard Yellow
Mountains	8" x 8" Light Purple 8" x 8" Dark Purple
Windows & Snow	8" x 8" White
Tree Trunks	⅛ Yard Brown
Faces	6" x 6" Flesh
Sun	6" x 6" Yellow
Sky	Fat Quarter Light Blue
Appliqué Base	½ Yard Solid Black
Paper-Backed Fusible Web	3 Yards
Backing	¾ Yard Blue
Batting	26" x 48" Batting
Binding	⅓ Yard Black
Additional Supplies	60" Measuring Tape

PREPARE THE APPLIQUÉ PATTERN by printing 11car_grwth_fit.pdf from the ladybugpatterns folder on the CD.

Select Fit to Printable Area from the Page Scaling drop down menu. (See detailed printing instructions, pages 21–22.)

Tape the pages together according to the diagram. Trim the excess white border from adjoining pages as necessary.

1	2
3	4
5	6
7	8

Background

Cut 1 rectangle 20" x 42" of dark blue.

Appliqués

Make all appliqués for the growth chart. (Refer to the Easy OutLine Appliqué Technique, pages 12–14.)

Remember that all appliqué patterns are printed in mirror image so they will be the same direction as the photo when the chart is complete.

There are 2 separate black silhouette appliqués for this chart.

One appliqué includes the entire scene on the growth chart and also forms the narrow black border.

One appliqué is the wheel to mark your child's height. Make as many of these as you want to have ready.

Use the photo to complete the appliqué scene. Remove the paper backing from the fusible on the base and fuse it to the dark blue background following the manufacturer's instructions.

The 2 appliqué bases look like this.

Finishing the Growth Chart

Quilting

Layer the growth chart, batting, and backing. The batting and backing should be several inches bigger than the chart on all 4 sides.

Quilt by hand or machine. Trim the batting and backing even with the chart top.

Stitch around the outside edge of the marker(s).

Trim the batting and backing even with the growth chart and marker(s).

Binding

Cut 3 strips 2½" wide of black and join end-to-end.

Press the binding strip in half lengthwise. Use this binding strip and your favorite method to bind the growth chart. We prefer a mitered binding (page 17).

Cut off the first 21½" of the tape measure.

Position the tape measure on the chart and use pins to hold it in place as shown. You do not want to put the pins through the tape measure because the holes will be permanent.

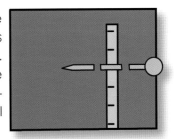

Sew the tape measure in place along both sides with a machine basting stitch.

Using the Growth Chart

Hang the growth chart so that the 21½" mark on the tape measure is 21½" from the floor.

Mark your child's height with a pin.

Write your child's name and the date on one of the markers. Sew the marker to the quilt with the arrow touching the appropriate spot on the tape measure.

Finished size 16" x 16"

Car or Truck
Throw Pillow

REFERENCE INSTRUCTIONS

Easy OutLine Appliqué Technique
(page 12)

Read all instructions before starting.

Use ¼" seam allowance except where noted.

MATERIALS

Pillow Front & Back	½ Yard Green Print For Each Pillow
Car Appliqué	
Car	Fat Quarter Turquoise
Windows & Headlight Rim	8" x 5" White
Wheel Spokes, Door Handle, Sky Border	9" x 9" Red
Wheels	11" x 7" Grey
Headlight	2" x 2" Yellow
Face	4" x 3" Flesh
Hair	3" x 3" Brown
Sky	6" x 6" Light Blue
Truck Appliqué	
Truck, Hat	Fat Quarter Red
Windows, Headlight Rim	8" x 5" White
Wheel Spokes, Door Handle, Sky Border	9"x 12" Turquoise
Wheels	11" x 7" Grey
Headlight	2" x 2" Yellow
Face	4" x 3" Flesh
Sky	6" x 6" Light Blue
Appliqué Base	15" x 15" Solid Black for Each Pillow
Pillow Form	16" x 16" for Each Pillow
Low-Loft Batting	24" x 42" for Each Pillow
Backing	⅔ Yard Muslin for Each Pillow
Paper-Backed Fusible Web	1 Yard for Each Pillow

PREPARE THE APPLIQUÉ PATTERN by printing 12car_pill_fit.pdf from the ladybugpatterns folder on the CD.

Select Fit to Printable Area from the Page Scaling drop down menu. (See detailed printing instructions, pages 21–22.)

Tape the pages together according to the diagram. Trim the excess white border from adjoining pages as necessary.

1	2	3
4	5	6

Appliqués

Make all appliqués for the pillows. (Refer to the Easy OutLine Appliqué Technique, pages 12–14.)

Remember that all appliqué patterns are printed in mirror image so they will be the same direction as the photo when the pillow is complete.

After making all the appliqués remove the paper backing from the fusible.

The 2 appliqué bases look like this.

Making the Pillow Front and Back

The pillow front and back are made by folding a single piece of fabric.

Cut 1 rectangle 17" x 38" of green print.

Fold in half and place a pin to mark the center on both sides of the rectangle.

Measure 7¾" up from each pin. Mark with a pin on both sides.

Measure 7¾" down from each pin. Mark with a pin on both sides.

Fold each end, right sides together, at the second and third set of pins. Press the fold.

This marks the area where you will place the appliqué.

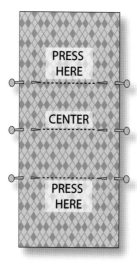

Position and fuse the appliqués in place following the manufacturer's instructions.

Quilting the Pillow

Layer the appliquéd pillow top with the batting and backing fabric. Quilt by hand or machine. Trim batting and backing even with the pillow top.

Fold under ½" at both short ends and top stitch.

Fold right sides together on the press lines, forming an overlap.

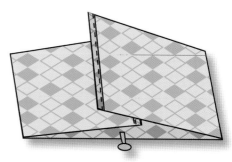

Fold on the press lines. Pin is marking the center.

Stitch down both sides with a ½" seam allowance.

Stitch both sides using ½" seams.

Turn right-side out and press the side seams flat.

Stuff the pillow form inside the pillow.

Finished size 26" x 26½"

Boy or Girl in a Car Wallhanging

REFERENCE INSTRUCTIONS

Easy OutLine Appliqué Technique
(page 12)

Basic Border Directions
(page 15)

Mitered Binding Directions
(page 17)

Read all instructions before starting.

Strips are cut selvage to selvage. Use ¼" seam allowance.

MATERIALS—BOY QUILT	
Sky	Fat Quarter Light Blue
Border	½ Yard Dark Blue
Road	¼ Yard Yellow
Bumper, Car Details, Dog Eyebrows & Nose	24" x 7" Orange
Car	Fat Quarter Red
Wheels, Headlights, Steering Wheel, Mirror	Fat Quarter Grey
Dog Body & Face	Fat Quarter Brown
Dog Face	6" x 6" Dark Brown
Dog Tongue, Boy Lips	4" x 4" Light Pink
Windows, Eyes	Fat Quarter White
Shirt, Hat, Car Details	Fat Quarter Light Green
Face	9" x 11" Flesh
Inside of Mouths	4" x 4" Fuchsia
Headlights	4" x 8" Yellow
Bill of Hat	7" x 3" Dark Green
Appliqué Base	¾ Yard Solid Black
Paper-Backed Fusible Web	3 Yards
Binding, Narrow Border	⅓ Yard Black
Batting	1 Yard
Backing	1 Yard

PREPARE THE APPLIQUÉ PATTERN by printing 13car_bygrl_fit.pdf from the ladybugpatterns folder on the CD.

Select Fit to Printable Area from the Page Scaling drop down menu. (See detailed printing instructions, pages 21–22.)

Tape the pages together according to the diagram. Trim the excess white border from adjoining pages as necessary.

1	2	3	4
5	6	7	8
9	10	11	12

Appliqués

Make all appliqués for the quilt. (Refer to the Easy Out-Line Appliqué Technique, pages12–14.)

After making the quilt background, remove the paper backing from the fusible and fuse the appliqués in place following the manufacturer's instructions. Refer to the photo for placement.

The appliqué base looks like this.

MATERIALS—GIRL QUILT	
Sky	Fat Quarter White Print
Border	½ Yard Lime Green
Road	¼ Yard Light Orange
Bumper, Bill of Hat	24" x 7" Dark Green
Car	Fat Quarter Pink
Wheels	5" x 8" Dark Grey
Dog Eyebrows & Nose, Steering Wheel	5" x 8" Orange
Dog Tongue, Girl Lips	4" x 4" Light Pink
Window, Headlights	Fat Quarter White
Hair	7" x 7" Orange Stripe
Face	9" x 11" Flesh
Inside of Mouths, Rim of Car Hood	Fat Quarter Fuchsia
Hat, Shirt	9" x 10" Green Print
Dog Body, Car Details	Fat Quarter Light Turquoise
Dog Face, Mirror, Inside of Steering Wheel	12" x 12" Dark Turquoise
Appliqué Base	¾ Yard Solid Black
Paper-Backed Fusible Web	3 Yards
Binding, Narrow Border	⅓ Yard Black
Batting	1 Yard
Backing	1 Yard

Quilt Background

Quilt Center

Cut 1 rectangle 17½" x 16¾" of light blue (boy) or white (girl).

Border 1

Cut 1 strip 2½" x 16 ¾" of dark blue (boy) or lime green (girl) and add to the left side of the quilt center.

Cut 1 strip 7½" x 16¾" of dark blue (boy) or lime green (girl) and add to the right side.

Cut 1 strip 2½" x 26½" of dark blue (boy) or lime green (girl) and add to the top.

Cut 1 strip 26½" x 1" of black (boy) or black & white stripe (girl) and add to the bottom.

Border 2

Cut 1 strip 26½" x 7¼" of yellow (boy) or orange (girl) and add to the bottom of the quilt.

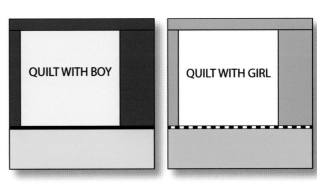

Fuse the appliqués in place.

Finishing the Quilt

Layer the appliquéd quilt top over the batting and backing fabric.

Quilt by hand or machine.

Cut 3 strips 2½" wide of black (boy) or black & white stripe (girl) for the binding and join end-to-end. Press the binding strip in half lengthwise. Use this binding strip and your favorite method to bind the quilt. We prefer a mitered binding (page 17).

Girly Fun

Finished size 40" x 52"

Baby Quilt

REFERENCE
INSTRUCTIONS

Basic Nine-Patch
Quilt Pattern
(page 5)

Border with Cornerstones
Directions
(page 16)

Mitered Binding Instructions
(page 17)

Strips are cut selvage to selvage.
Use ¼" seam allowance.

Materials	
Block 1	⅔ Yard Yellow Flower Print
Block 2	⅝ Yard Green Print FABRIC A
	½ Yard Pink Print FABRIC B
Block 2 centers & cornerstones	⅓ Yard Blue Print FABRIC C
Border 1 & Binding	⅝ Yard Pink Stripe
Border 2	⅝ Yard Green Print
Batting	49" x 61"
Backing	1¾ Yards Pink

Block 1

Cut 3 strips 6½" wide of large flower print.

Cut 17 blocks 6½" x 6½" from the strips.

17 blocks

Block 2—Nine Patch

Cut 7 strips 2½" of green (FABRIC A).

Cut 6 strips 2½" of pink (FABRIC B).

Cut 2 strips 2½" of blue (FABRIC C).

Make 18 Nine-Patch blocks.

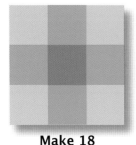

Make 18

Sew the Blocks Together

Sew the blocks together as shown to make 7 rows of 5 blocks each.

Make 4 rows like this.

Make 5 rows like this.

Sew the 7 rows together so that your quilt top has a checkerboard appearance.

Make the Borders

Measure both the length and width of the quilt top before cutting the borders.

Border 1
Cut 4 strips 1½" wide of pink stripe.

Add Border 1 to all 4 sides of the quilt. (See detailed Border instructions on page 15.)

Border 2
Cut 4 strips 4½" wide of green and join end-to-end.

Measure the width of the quilt before adding Border 2. Width = _____

Add Border 2 to the sides.

Cut 4 squares 4½" x 4½" of blue (FABRIC C) for the cornerstones.

Cut 2 strips equal to the width measurement noted above. Sew a 4½" x 4½" blue cornerstone to both ends of each strip. Press the seams toward the border strips.

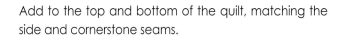

Add to the top and bottom of the quilt, matching the side and cornerstone seams.

Finishing the Quilt

Layer quilt, batting, and backing. The batting and backing should be several inches bigger than the quilt on all 4 sides.

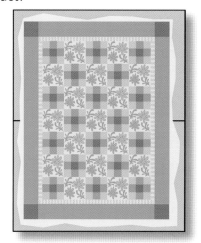

Quilt by hand or machine. Trim the batting and backing even with the quilt top.

Cut 5 strips 2½" wide of pink stripe for the binding and join end-to-end.

Press the binding strip in half lengthwise. Use this binding strip and your favorite method to bind the quilt. We prefer a mitered binding (page 17).

Quilting Suggestion

The Carla's Cutom Feathers quilting design is available at our website, www.quiltedfrog.com/shop/category/quilting-designs-by-quilted-frog/

REFERENCE INSTRUCTIONS

Basic Pillowcase Pattern
(page 8)

Easy OutLine Appliqué Technique
(page 12)

Read all instructions before starting.

This pillowcase is a little different Cuff A is pieced.

MATERIALS

Cuff A Wall	¼ Yard Pink Stripe
Cuff A Floor, Cuff B, Cuff C	⅝ Yard Yellow Print
Borders	⅛ Yard Green Check
Pillowcase Body	⅔ Yard Pink, Blue & Yellow Print, or Solid
Face, Letters on Blocks	6" x 6" Light Brown
Collar, Blocks, Ball Stripe	6" x 6" Dark Pink
Jacks	6" x 6" Dark Turquoise
Baby Buggy	9" x 9" Blue
Baby Buggy Handle & Trim	6" x 6" Brown
Dress	3" x 5" Green
Ball	4" x 4" Dark Green
Name	6" x 14" Medium Green
Wheels	2 – 2" Brown Buttons, 2 – 1⅜" Blue Buttons 2 – 1" Tortoise Shell Buttons
Ball	3 – ¼" Yellow Buttons
Eyes	2 – ¼" Blue Buttons
Appliqué Base	Fat Quarter Solid Black
Lightweight Batting	26" x 16"
Paper-Backed Fusible Web	¾ Yard

Finished size 21" x 31½"

Baby Carriage Pillowcase

PREPARE THE APPLIQUÉ PATTERN by printing14crrg_case_fit.pdf and the 25alphabet.pdf from the ladybugpatterns folder on the CD.

Select Fit to Printable Area from the Page Scaling drop down menu. (See detailed printing instructions, pages 21–22.)

Tape the pages together according to the diagram at right. Trim the excess white border from adjoining pages as necessary.

Appliqués

Make all appliqués for the pillowcase. (Refer to the Easy OutLine Appliqué Technique, pages 12–14.)

Appliqué patterns are printed in mirror image so they will be the same direction as the photo when the pillowcase is complete.

After making all the appliqués remove the paper backing from the fusible.

The 4 appliqué bases look like this.

Use the alphabet appliqué patterns (25alphabet_fit.pdf) to personalize the pillowcase if you wish. If the name you want to use is too long to fit, reduce the size of the letter patterns on a copy machine.

Pillowcase Cuff

Cuff A
Cut 1 strip 22" x 7½" of pink stripe.
Cut 1 strip 22" x 1" of green check.
Cut 1 strip 22" x 3" of yellow print.

Sew the 3 pieces together to make Cuff A.

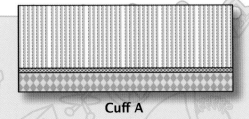

Cuff A

Position the appliqués on Cuff A and fuse in place. Use the original pattern and picture of the finished pillowcase as placement guides.

Layer the batting with Cuff A with the fused appliqués right-side up. Pin or baste the 2 layers together and quilt by machine. Trim the quilted Cuff A to measure 21½" x 8½".

Stack the brown, blue, and tortoise shell buttons and sew in place for the carriage wheels.

Cut a strip 21½" x 8½" of yellow print for Cuff B. Cut 1 strip 43" x 8½" yellow print for Cuff C.

Finish the cuff according to the Basic Pllowcase instructions (page 8).

Pillowcase Body

Square up the cut edges of the ⅔ yard pillowcase body fabric.

Cut a border strip 1¼" wide of green check fabric. Sew to the top edge of the body.

Cut off the selvages and trim the body and cuff to the same width.

Fold the body in half, aligning the selvage-trimmed edges, right sides together. Sew the long sides and the end opposite the border strip. Turn the body right-side out. Press flat.

Complete the Cuff

Join the short ends of the cuff unit and press the seam open.

Fold the cuff in half along the long seam, wrong sides together with the appliqué facing out.

Baste the raw edges together by machine or hand.

Sew Cuff to Body

Join the cuff to the border on the body according to the instructions on page 11.

Turn the cuff right-side out and press the seam flat.

Your pillowcase is complete and ready to use.

REFERENCE INSTRUCTIONS

Basic Pillowcase Pattern
(page 8)

Easy OutLine Appliqué Technique
(page 12)

Read all instructions before starting.

MATERIALS

Cuff A, Cuff B & Cuff C	⅔ Yard Pink
Border	⅛ Yard Pink Stripe
Pillowcase Body	⅔ Yard Pink Print or Solid
Body	Fat Quarter Blue
Nose	3" x 3" Dark Blue
Ears, Eyes, Crown	5" x 6" Purple
Eyes	2" x 2" White
Mirror, Collar, Details	6" x 14" Yellow
Mirror Frame, Tongue	6" x 10" Dark Red
Appliqué Base	Fat Quarter Solid Black
Lightweight Batting	26" x 16"
Paper-Backed Fusible Web	¾ yard

Finished size 21½" x 31½"

Princess Kitty Pillowcase

PREPARE THE APPLIQUÉ PATTERN by printing 15ktty_case_fit.pdf from the ladybugpatterns folder on the CD.

Select Fit to Printable Area from the Page Scaling drop down menu. (See detailed printing instructions, pages 21–22.)

Tape the pages together according to the diagram. Trim the excess white border from adjoining pages as necessary.

Appliqués

Make all appliqués for the pillowcase. (Refer to the Easy OutLine Appliqué Technique, pages 12–14.)

Remember that all appliqué patterns are printed in mirror image so they will be the same direction as the photo when the pillowcase is complete.

After making all the appliqués remove the paper backing from the fusible.

The appliqué base looks like this.

Pillowcase Cuff

Note: Fabric widths can vary from 40"–44" wide. Make certain you use no more than half the fabric width for Cuff A and Cuff B.

Cut 1 strip 22" x 10" of pink for Cuff A.

Position the appliqués on Cuff A. Use the original pattern and picture of the finished pillowcase as placement guides. Make sure that the black horizon line of the appliqué aligns with the seam. Fuse the appliqués in place following the fusible manufacturer's instructions.

Layer the batting with Cuff A, with the fused appliqués right-side up. Pin or baste the 2 layers together and quilt by machine. Trim the quilted Cuff A to measure 21½" x 9½".

Cut 1 strip 21½"x 9½" of pink for Cuff B. Cut 1 strip 43" x 9" of pink for Cuff C.

Finish the cuff according to the Basic Pillowcase instructions (pages 8–11).

Pillowcase Body

Square up the cut edges of the ⅔ yard pillowcase body fabric.

Cut 1 border strip 1" wide of pink stripe fabric. Sew to the top edge of the body.

Cut off the selvages and trim the body and cuff to the same width.

Fold the body in half, aligning the selvage-trimmed edges, right sides together. Sew the long sides and the end opposite the border with a ¼" seam. Turn the body right-side out. Press flat.

Complete the cuff

Join the short ends of the cuff unit and press the seam open.

Fold the cuff in half along the long seam with the wrong sides of the fabric together and the appliqué facing out.

Baste the raw edges together by machine or hand.

Sew Cuff to Body

Join the cuff and the body according to the instructions on page 11.

Turn the cuff right-side out and press the seam flat.

Your pillowcase is complete and ready to use.

Things That Go

REFERENCE INSTRUCTIONS

Basic Pillowcase Pattern
(page 8)

Easy OutLine Appliqué Technique
(page 12)

Read all instructions before starting.

The cuff for this pillowcase is a little different from the basic pillowcase. Cuff A is pieced from two rectangles to create the sky and ground.

MATERIALS	
Cuff A Sky	¼ Yard Blue Print
Cuff A Ground, Cuff B, Cuff C	⅝ yard Green Stripe
Border 1	⅛ yard Black & White Stripe
Border 2	1" x 22" Dark Blue
Pillowcase Body	⅔ Yard Red
Faces	4" x 4" Each 4 Different Browns
Truck	6" x 8" Green
Flame, Headlights	6" x 8" Yellow
Wheels & Axles	6" x 8" Grey
Wheel Spokes, Car Detail	6" x 6" Red
Cars	4" x 5" Each Turquoise, Orange, Purple
Windows	6"x 6" White
Appliqué Base	22" x 10" Solid Black
Lightweight Batting	26" x 16"
Paper-Backed Fusible Web	⅔ Yard

Finished size 21½" x 31½"

Monster Truck Pillowcase

PREPARE THE APPLIQUÉ PATTERN by printing 16trck_case_fit.pdf from the ladybugpatterns folder on the CD.

Select Fit to Printable Area from the Page Scaling drop down menu. (See detailed printing instructions, pages 21–22.)

Tape the pages together according to the diagram. Trim the excess white border from adjoining pages as necessary.

Appliqués

Make all appliqués for the pillowcase. (Refer to the Easy OutLine Appliqué Technique, pages 12–14.)

The appliqué includes the details of the picture.

Remember that all appliqué patterns are printed in mirror image so they will be the same direction as the photo when the pillowcase is complete.

After making all the appliqués remove the paper backing from the fusible.

The 4 appliqué bases look like this.

Pillowcase Cuff

Cut 1 strip 22" x 5" of blue for Cuff A Sky.
Cut 1 strip 22" x 6" of green stripe for Cuff A Ground.

Place right sides together and sew the long sides together. Press the seam toward the green stripe section.

Position the appliqués on Cuff A. Use the original pattern and picture of the finished pillowcase as placement guides. Make sure that the appliqué covers the seam. Fuse the appliqués in place following the fusible manufacturer's instructions.

Layer the batting with Cuff A, with the fused appliqués right-side up. Pin or baste the 2 layers together and quilt by machine. Trim the quilted Cuff A to measure 21½" x 10".

Cut 1 strip 21½" x 10" of green stripe for Cuff B. Cut one 43" x 10" piece of green stripe fabric for Cuff C.

Finish the cuff according to the Basic Pillowcase instructions (pages 8–11).

Pillowcase Body

Square up the cut edges of the ⅔ yard pillowcase body fabric.

Cut 1 border strip 1¼" wide of black & white stripe fabric. Sew to the top edge of the body.

Cut off the selvages and trim the body and cuff to the same width.

Fold the body in half, aligning the selvage-trimmed edges, right sides together. Sew the long sides and the end opposite the border with a ¼" seam. Turn the body right-side out. Press flat.

Complete the Cuff

Join the short ends of the cuff unit and press the seam open.

Fold the cuff in half along the long seam with the wrong sides of the fabric together and the appliqué facing out.

Baste the raw edges together by machine or hand.

Sew Cuff to Body

Join the cuff and the body according to the instructions on page 11.

Turn the cuff right-side out and press the seam flat.

Your pillowcase is complete and ready to use.

Finished size 42" x 18"

Monster Truck Wallhanging

REFERENCE INSTRUCTIONS

Basic Border Directions
(page 15)

Easy OutLine Appliqué Technique
(page 12)

Mitered Binding Instructions
(page 17)

Read all instructions before starting.

Strips are cut selvage to selvage unless otherwise noted. Use ¼" seam allowance.

MATERIALS

Road	¼ Yard Green Stripe
Sky	¼ Yard Blue Print
Faces – Boy & Dad	Fat Quarter Flesh
Dad's Hair	5" x 7" Medium Brown
Small Faces of Crowd	5" x 5" of 4 or 5 Different Browns
Truck, Eyes	6" x 8" Green
Flame, Headlights, Flag, Dad's Hat	Fat Quarter Yellow
Wheels	7" x 9" Grey
Wheel Spokes, Car Detail, Flags, Dad's Shirt	Fat Quarter Red
Car, Flag, Boy's Shirt	Fat Quarter Orange
Cars	5" x 5" Each Turquoise and Purple
Flags	6" x 18" Black & White Check
Windows	8" x 8" White
Borders 1, 3, Binding	½ Yard Black & White Stripe
Border 2	1" x 42" Dark Blue
Border 4	⅓ Yard Medium Blue
Appliqué Base	½ Yard Solid Black
Paper-Backed Fusible Web	2 Yards
Batting	⅔ Yard
Backing	⅔ Yard Blue

PREPARE THE APPLIQUÉ PATTERN by printing 17trck_wall_fit.pdf from the ladybugpatterns folder on the CD.

Select Fit to Printable Area from the Page Scaling drop down menu. (See detailed printing instructions, pages 21–22.)

Tape the pages together according to the diagram. Trim the excess white border from adjoining pages as necessary.

1	2	3
4	5	6

Quilt Background, Borders 1 & 2

Cut 1 strip 4½" x 38½" of blue print for the Sky.

Cut 1 strip 38½ x 1¼" of black & white stripe for Border 1.

Cut 1 strip 38½" x 1" of dark blue for Border 2.

Cut 1 strip 38½" x 4" of green stripe for the Road.

Join the 4 strips as shown.

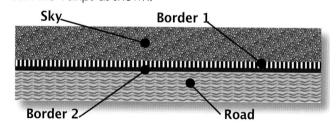

Sky — Border 1 — Border 2 — Road

Borders 3, 4 & Flags

Border 3
Cut 2 strips 1" x 38½" and sew to the top and bottom of quilt.

Cut 2 strips 1" x 10¼" and sew to the sides of the quilt.

Flags

Make 2 black & white check, 1 yellow, 1 red, and 1 orange flag.

For each flag cut 2 triangles using the flag pattern.

Place matching triangles right sides together and stitch on the dotted line with a ¼" seam.

Turn the flags right-side out and press.

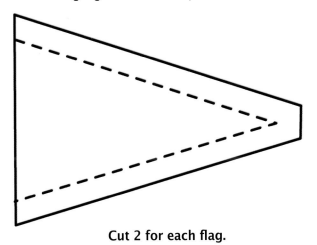

Cut 2 for each flag.

Pin the flags to the bottom of the quilt as shown. Place the first flag 1½" from the left edge and the other flags ¾" apart.

Border 4

Cut all the Border 4 strips from the blue.

Cut 1 strip 3½" x 38½" and sew to the top of the quilt.

Cut 1 strip 5½" x 38½" and sew to the bottom of the quilt.

Cut 2 strips 2" x 18¼" and sew to the sides.

Press the flags down after sewing on the borders.

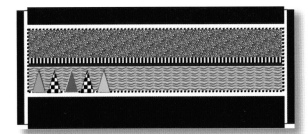

Appliqués

Make all appliqués for the quilt. (Refer to the Easy Out-Line Appliqué Technique, pages 12–14.)

Remember that all appliqué patterns are printed in mirror image so they will be the same direction as the photo when the quilt is complete.

After making all the appliqués remove the paper backing from the fusible. Fuse in place following the manufacturer's instructions. Refer to the photo for placement.

You will make 5 separate appliqués for this quilt.

One is the boy, the father, and the monster truck.
One is the spectators in the stands.
and three are the little cars.

The 5 appliqué bases look like this.

Finishing the Quilt

Quilting

Layer the quilt, batting, and backing. The batting and backing should be several inches bigger than the quilt on all 4 sides.

Quilt by hand or machine. Trim the batting and backing even with the quilt top.

Binding

Cut 3 strips 2½" wide of the black & white stripe for the binding and join end-to-end.

Press the binding strip in half lengthwise. Use this binding strip and your favorite method to bind the quilt. We prefer a mitered binding (page 17).

Animal Fun

REFERENCE INSTRUCTIONS

Basic Pillowcase Pattern
(page 8)

Easy OutLine Appliqué Technique
(page 12)

Read all instructions before starting.

MATERIALS

Cuff	⅔ Yard Gold
Border	⅛ Yard Blue & Green Stripe
Pillowcase Body	⅔ Yard Green Print
Alligator Body	Fat Quarter Dark Green
Alligator Spots & Tummy	9" x 5" Light Green
Bird Body, Alligator Eyes	5" x 5" Blue
Bird Wing	2" x 2" Dark Blue
Highlight in Eyes	2" x 2" White
Bird Eyes, Alligator Nose	3" x 3" Pink
Bird Beak	2" x 2" Orange
Appliqué Base	Fat Quarter Solid Black
Teeth	½ Yard Jumbo White Rickrack
Lightweight Batting	28" x 16"
Paper-Backed Fusible Web	1 yard

Finished size 21½" x 31½"

Alligator Pillowcase

PREPARE THE APPLIQUÉ PATTERN by printing 18gatr_case_fit.pdf from the ladybugpatterns folder on the CD.

Select Fit to Printable Area from the Page Scaling drop down menu. (See detailed printing instructions, pages 21–22.)

Tape the pages together according to the diagram. Trim the excess white border from adjoining pages as necessary.

1	2

Appliqués

Make all appliqués for the pillowcase. (Refer to the *Easy OutLine Appliqué* Technique, pages 12–14.)

Remember that all appliqué patterns are printed in mirror image so they will be the same direction as the photo when the pillowcase is complete.

The appliqué base looks like this.

Alligator Head

Before fusing the green piece for the alligator's head to the black base, cut out the mouth area that is marked in gray on the pattern.

Position the rickrack teeth in the mouth and sew in place.

Fuse the head with the teeth to the black base. Before fusing the complete appliqué to the cuff, stitch around the mouth again. Try to stitch over the same stitches you made before.

After making all the appliqués remove the paper backing from the fusible.

Pillowcase Cuff

Note: Fabric widths can vary from 40"–44" wide. Make certain you use no more than half the fabric width for Cuff A and Cuff B.

Cut 1 strip 24" x 12" of gold for Cuff A.

Position the appliqués on Cuff A. Use the original pattern and picture of the finished pillowcase as placement guides. Fuse the appliqués in place following the fusible manufacturer's instructions.

Layer the batting with Cuff A, with the fused appliqués right-side up. Pin or baste the 2 layers together and quilt by machine. Trim the quilted Cuff A to measure 21½" x 8½".

Cut 1 strip 21½" x 8½" piece of gold for Cuff B. Cut 1 strip 8½" x 43" of gold for Cuff C.

Finish the cuff according to the Basic Pillowcase instructions (pages 8–11).

Pillowcase Body

Square up the cut edges of the ⅔ yard pillowcase body fabric.

Cut 1 border strip ¼" wide of blue stripe fabric. Sew to the top edge of the body.

Cut off the selvages and trim the body and cuff to the same width.

Fold the body in half, aligning the selvage-trimmed edges, right sides together. Sew the long sides and the end opposite the border with a ¼" seam. Turn the body right-side out. Press flat.

Complete the Cuff

Join the short ends of the cuff unit and press the seam open.

Fold the cuff in half along the long seam with the wrong sides of the fabric together and the appliqué facing out.

Baste the raw edges together by machine or hand.

Sew Cuff to Body

Join the cuff and the body according to the instructions on page 11.

Turn the cuff right-side out and press the seam flat.

Your pillowcase is complete and ready to use.

Strips are cut selvage to selvage unless otherwise noted.
Use ¼" seam allowance.

MATERIALS

Cuff	⅔ Yard Orange
Borders	⅛ Yard Green & Blue Stripe
Pillowcase Body	⅔ Yard Bright Green Print or Solid Fabric
Frog	Fat Quarter Bright Green
Frog Spots	3" x 3" Pink
Frog Eyes	1" x 1" White
Lily Pads	12" x 6" Dark Green
Flower	9" x 8" Pink
Bug Wings	3" x 3" Purple
Bug Head	2" x 2" Blue
Antennae	1" x 1" Pink
Appliqué Base	Fat Quarter Solid Black
Lightweight Batting	26" x 16"
Paper-Backed Fusible Web	1 Yard
Fly Path	Pink Embroidery Floss

Finished size 21½" x 31½"

Leap Frog Pillowcase

PREPARE THE APPLIQUÉ PATTERN by printing 19frog_case_fit.pdf from the ladybugpatterns folder on the CD.

Select Fit to Printable Area from the Page Scaling drop down menu. (See detailed printing instructions, pages 21–22.)

Tape the pages together according to the diagram. Trim the excess white border from adjoining pages as necessary.

Appliqués

Make all appliqués for the pillowcase. (Refer to the Easy OutLine Appliqué Technique, pages 12–14.)

Remember that all appliqué patterns are printed in mirror image so they will be the same direction as the photo when the pillowcase is complete.

After making all the appliqués remove the paper backing from the fusible.

Embroider the bug's path with embroidery floss.

The 2 appliqué bases look like this.

Pillowcase Cuff

Note: Fabric widths can vary from 40"–44" wide. Make certain you use no more than half the fabric width for Cuff A and Cuff B.

Cut 1 strip 22" x 12" of orange fabric for Cuff A.

Position the appliqués on Cuff A. Use the original pattern and picture of the finished pillowcase as placement guides. Fuse the appliqués in place following the fusible manufacturer's instructions.

Layer the batting with Cuff A, with the fused appliqués right-side up. Pin or baste the 2 layers together and quilt by machine. Trim the quilted Cuff A to measure 21½" x 9".

Cut 1 strip 21½" x 9" of orange fabric for Cuff B.

Join a short end of the quilted Cuff A with unquilted Cuff B, right sides together. Press the seam open.

Border

From the stripe fabric, cut: 1 strip 1¼" wide.
1 strip 2" wide.

Sew the 1¼" wide strip to the top edge of the Cuff A/Cuff B unit.

Sew the 2" wide strip to the bottom edge of the Cuff A/Cuff B unit.

Cut 1 strip 43" x 9¾" of orange fabric for Cuff C.

Sew Cuff C to the bottom of the Cuff A/Cuff B unit. Press the seam open.

Pillowcase Body

Square up the cut edges of the ⅔ yard pillowcase body fabric.

Cut off the selvages and trim the body and cuff to the same width.

Fold the body in half, aligning the selvage-trimmed edges, right sides together. Sew the long sides and the end opposite the border with a ¼" seam. Turn the body right-side out. Press flat.

Complete the cuff

Join the short ends of the cuff unit and press the seam open.

Fold the cuff in half along the bottom border seam with the wrong sides of the fabric together and the appliqué facing out.

Baste the raw edges together by machine or hand.

Sew Cuff to Body

Join the cuff and the body according to the instructions on page 11. Turn the cuff right-side out and press the seam flat. Your pillowcase is complete and ready to use.

REFERENCE INSTRUCTIONS

Basic Pillowcase Pattern
(page 8)

Easy OutLine Appliqué Technique
(page 12)

Read all instructions before starting.

This pillowcase is a little different. Cuff A is pieced.

MATERIALS

Cuff A Sky, Cuff B, Cuff C	¾ Yard Blue
Cuff A Ground	12" x 14" Green
Border	⅛ Yard Red
	⅛ Yard Green Stripe
Pillowcase Body	⅔ Yard Green & Black Print or Solid
Dinosaur Body	Fat Quarter Orange Spot
Dinosaur Spots, Bird Top Knot, Feathers	7" x 7" Light Green
Dinosaur Eyes	3" x 3" White
Bird	4" x 6" Dark Red
Beak	2" x 2" Yellow
Appliqué Base	Fat Quarter Solid Black
Lightweight Batting	26" x 16"
Paper-Backed Fusible Web	⅔ Yard

Finished size 21½" x 31½"

Dinosaur Pillowcase

PREPARE THE APPLIQUÉ & CUFF PATTERNS by printing 20dino_case_fit.pdf from the ladybugpatterns folder on the CD.

Select Fit to Printable Area from the Page Scaling drop down menu. (See detailed printing instructions, pages 21–22.)

Tape the pages together according to the diagram. Trim the excess white border from adjoining pages as necessary.

1	2
3	4
5	6
7	8

Appliqués

Make all appliqués for the pillowcase. (Refer to the Easy OutLine Appliqué Technique, pages 12–14.)

Remember that all appliqué patterns are printed in mirror image so they will be the same direction as the photo when the pillowcase is complete.

After making all the appliqués remove the paper backing from the fusible.

The appliqué base looks like this.

Pillowcase Cuff

The Cuff A section is pieced before fusing the appliqués to it. The pattern pieces are a little larger than the finished Cuff A measurements to allow for take-up while quilting. It is trimmed to the correct size after quilting.

Cut 1 Cuff A—Sky of blue fabric.
Cut 1 Cuff A—Ground of green fabric.

With right sides together, match the notches and sew together with a ¼" seam. The seam line is marked on the pattern pieces with a dotted line. Press the seam toward the green fabric.

Place all of the appliqués on Cuff A. Use the original pattern and picture of the finished pillowcase as placement guides. Fuse the appliqués in place following the fusible manufacturer's instructions.

Layer the batting with Cuff A, with the fused appliqués right-side up. Pin or baste the 2 layers together and quilt by machine. Trim the quilted cuff to measure 21½" x 10½".

Cut 1 strip 21½"x 10½" of blue for Cuff B. Cut 1 strip 43" x 10½" of blue for Cuff C.

Finish the cuff according to the Basic Pillowcase instructions (page 8–11).

Pillowcase Body

Square up the cut edges of the ⅔ yard pillowcase body fabric.

Cut 2 border strips 1" wide of red.
Cut 1 border strip 1½" of green stripe.

Sew a red strip to each side of the green striped strip. Press the seams toward the green stripe. Sew to the top edge of the body.

Cut off the selvages and trim the body and cuff to the same width.

Fold the body in half, aligning the selvage-trimmed edges, right sides together. Sew the long sides and the end opposite the border strip. Turn the body right-side out. Press flat.

Complete the Cuff

Join the short ends of the cuff unit and press the seam open.

Fold the cuff in half along the long seam, wrong sides together with the appliqué facing out.

Baste the raw edges together by machine or hand.

Sew Cuff to Body

Join the cuff to the border on the body according to the instructions on page 11.

Turn the cuff right-side out and press the seam flat.

Your pillowcase is complete and ready to use.

REFERENCE INSTRUCTIONS

Basic Pillowcase Pattern
(page 8)

Easy OutLine Appliqué Technique
(page 12)

Read all instructions before starting.

This design is a little different. The entire Cuff A piece is a large appliqué.

Strips are cut selvage to selvage unless otherwise noted.
Use ¼" seam allowance.

MATERIALS

Cuff A (Appliqué Base)	½ Yard Solid Black
Pillowcase Body	⅔ Yard Red & White Print or Solid Fabric
Ants	9" x 9" Red
Pants Appliqués, Cuff B & Cuff C	¾ Yard Blue
Belt	23" x 2¼" Medium Brown
Buttons	4" x 4" Dark Brown
Eyes	4" x 4" Green
Lightweight Batting	26" x 16"
Paper-Backed Fusible Web	1 Yard

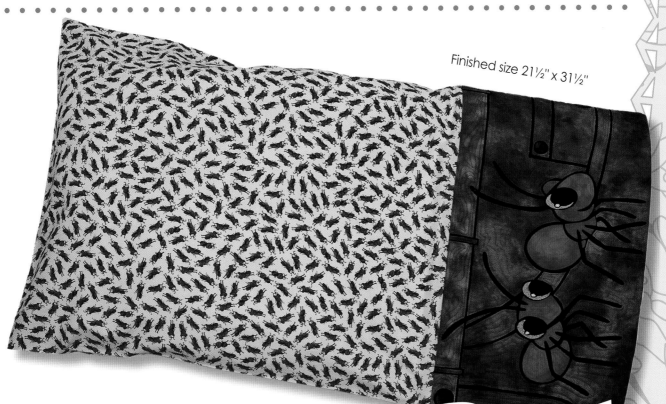

Finished size 21½" x 31½"

Ants in the Pants Pillowcase

PREPARE THE APPLIQUÉ PATTERN by printing 21ant_case_fit.pdf from the ladybugpatterns folder on the CD.

Select Fit to Printable Area from the Page Scaling drop down menu. (See detailed printing instructions, pages 21–22.)

Tape the pages together according to the diagram. Trim the excess white border from adjoining pages as necessary.

| 1 | 2 | 3 |
| 4 | 5 | 6 |

Appliqués

Make all appliqués for the pillowcase. (Refer to the Easy OutLine Appliqué Technique, pages 12–14.)

Make the pants with the belt as a single appliqué.

Make each ant as a separate appliqué and add them to the pants appliqué.

Remember that all appliqué patterns are printed in mirror image so they will be the same direction as the photo when the pillowcase is complete.

After making all the appliqués remove the paper backing from the fusible.

The 2 appliqué bases look like this.

Pillowcase Cuff

Cut 1 strip 22" x 13" of black for Cuff A, which is also the appliqué base.

Place all of the pants and belt pieces on the base. Position the ant appliqués on top. The grey dotted lines on the pants appliqué pattern show the placement of the ants. Leave a little black around all 4 edges so you have room to trim the finished cuff. Use the original pattern and picture of the finished pillowcase as placement guides.

Fuse the appliqués in place following the fusible manufacturer's instructions.

Layer the batting with Cuff A, with the fused appliqués right-side up. Pin or baste the 2 layers together and quilt by machine. Trim the quilted Cuff A to measure 21½" x 12½".

Cut 1 strip 21½" x 12½" of blue for Cuff B. Cut 1 strip 43" x 12" of blue for Cuff C.

Finish the cuff according to the Basic Pllowcase instructions (pages 8–11).

Pillowcase Body

Square up the cut edges of the ⅔ yard pillowcase body fabric.

Cut off the selvages and trim the body and cuff to the same width.

Fold the body in half, aligning the selvage-trimmed edges, right sides together. Sew the long sides and one end with a ¼" seam. Turn the body right-side out. Press flat.

Complete the Cuff

Join the short ends of the cuff unit and press the seam open.

Fold the cuff in half along the long seam with the wrong sides of the fabric together and the appliqué facing out.

Baste the raw edges together by machine or hand.

Sew Cuff to Body

Join the cuff and the body according to the instructions on page 11.

Turn the cuff right-side out and press the seam flat.

Your pillowcase is complete and ready to use.

Ants in the Pants
Wallhanging

Basic Border Directions
(page 15)

Easy OutLine Appliqué Technique
(page 12)

Mitered Binding Directions
(page 17)

Read all instructions before starting.

Strips are cut selvage to selvage unless otherwise noted. Use ¼" seam allowance.

MATERIALS

Background	Fat Quarter Yellow
Border 1, Binding	½ Yard Multicolor Stripe
Border 2	¼ Yard Green Print
Ants	6" x 8" Red
Pants	Fat Quarter Blue
Belt, Clothespins	8" x 12" Medium Brown
Buckle, Buttons	5" x 5" Dark Brown
Clothesline, Eye Highlights	3" x 6" White
Eyes	5" x 5" Green
Appliqué Base	½ Yard Black
Paper-Backed Fusible Web	1½ Yards
Buttons	3 – 1" Buttons
Batting	20" x 28"
Backing	⅔ Yard Blue or Green

PREPARE THE APPLIQUÉ PATTERN by printing 22ant_wall_fit.pdf from the ladybugpatterns folder on the CD.

Select Fit to Printable Area from the Page Scaling drop down menu. (See detailed printing instructions, pages 21–22.)

Tape the pages together according to the diagram. Trim the excess white border from adjoining pages as necessary.

```
1  2
3  4
5  6
```

Background

Cut 1 rectangle 11½" x 14½" of yellow.

Borders

Border 1
From the multicolor stripe, cut:
2 strips 1" x 14½".
2 strips 1½" x 12½".

Add the 14½" strips to the sides of the background and the 12½" strips to the top and bottom (page 15–16).

Border 2
Cut all Border 2 strips from the green print.

Cut 1 strip 2½" x 16½" and add to the left side of the quilt.

Cut 1 strip 1½" x 16½" and add to the right side of the quilt.

Cut 1 strip 15½" x 4" and add to the top.

Cut 1 strip 16½" x 5" and add to the bottom.

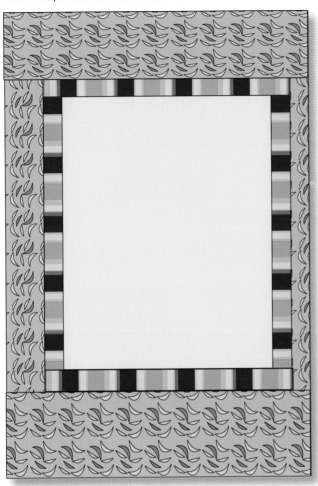

Appliqués

Make all appliqués for the quilt. (Refer to the Easy Out-Line Appliqué Technique, pages 12–14.)

One appliqué is the ant standing on the ground.

The other appliqué includes the rest of the picture.

Remember that all appliqué patterns are printed in mirror image so they will be the same direction as the photo when the quilt is complete.

After making all the appliqués remove the paper backing from the fusible. Position the appliqués on the quilt and fuse in place following the manufacturer's instructions. Use the photo as a placement guide.

The 5 appliqué bases look like this.

Finishing the Quilt

Quilting

Layer the quilt, batting, and backing. The batting and backing should be several inches bigger than the quilt on all 4 sides.

Quilt by hand or machine. Trim the batting and backing even with the quilt top.

Binding

Cut 3 strips 2½" wide of multicolor stripe and join end-to-end.

Press the binding strip in half lengthwise. Use this binding strip and your favorite method to bind the quilt. We prefer a mitered binding (page 17).

Things That Go Bump in the Night

Finished size 27" x 27" — Finished game pieces 9" x 9"

Monster Tic-Tac-Toe Game Quilt

REFERENCE INSTRUCTIONS

Basic 9-Patch Quilt pattern
(page 5)

Basic Border Directions
(page 15)

Easy Outline Appliqué Technique
(page 12)

Mitered Binding Directions
(page 17)

Bias Binding Directions
(page 20)

Read all instructions before starting.

These instructions are for 1 quilt and 10 game pieces.

Strips are cut selvage to selvage.
Use ¼" seam allowance.

MATERIALS

Quilt:

Center Block, Border 1, Border Squares	½ Yard Red Stripe
Four-Patch Blocks	Fat Quarter Each Green, Dark Blue, Yellow, and Purple
Corner Blocks	Fat Quarter Green Stripe
Block Borders, Border 2, Border 3, Quilt Binding	⅝ Yard Black Print

Monster Tic-Tac-Toe Pieces:

Monster Bodies & Legs	Fat Quarter Turquoise
Monster Bodies	Fat Quarter Red
Monster Legs	10" x 10" Dark Purple
Spots, Eyes, Toes	10" x 10" Green
Eye Highlights	6" x 6 White
Background	Fat Quarter Each Purple, Dark Blue, Yellow, and Orange
Appliqué Bases	1½ Yards Solid Black
Paper-Backed Fusible Web	3 Yards
Backing–Quilt	1 Yard Green Stripe
Backing–Tic-Tac-Toe Pieces	1½ Yards Green Stripe
Batting–Quilt	1 Yard
Batting–Tic-Tac-Toe Pieces	1½ Yards
Binding–Tic-Tac-Toe Pieces	1 Yard Black Print

PREPARE THE APPLIQUÉ PATTERN by printing 23mnst_game_fit.pdf from the ladybugpatterns folder on the CD.

Select Fit to Printable Area from the Page Scaling drop down menu. (See detailed printing instructions, pages 21–22.)

Tape the pages together according to the diagram. Trim the excess white border from adjoining pages as necessary.

1 2 3

Quilt Background

Four-Patch Blocks
Cut 4 squares 4¼" x 4¼" each from the yellow, green, purple, and dark blue (16 total).

Sew the squares together following the diagram to make 4 Four-Patch blocks.

Cut 4 strips ¾" wide of black print.

From these strips cut 8 segments 8" long and 8 segments 8½" long.

Make 4 of these blocks.

Add the 8" strips to the sides of the blocks and the 8½" strips to the top and bottom as shown.

Large Corner Blocks
Cut 4 squares 8½" x 8½" of green stripe.

Center Block
Cut 1 square 8½" x 8½" of red stripe.

Sew the quilt blocks together as shown.

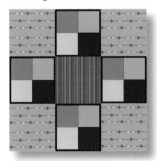

Borders

Border 1
Cut 4 strips ¾" wide of red stripe.

Add Border 1 to all 4 sides of the quilt. (See detailed Border instructions on page 15.)

Border 2
Cut 4 strips ⅞" wide of black print.

Add Border 2 to all 4 sides of the quilt.

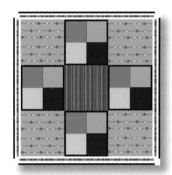

Border 3
Cut 3 strips 1½" wide of green.

From these strips cut:
4 strips 16⅛" x 1½" (A)
4 strips 2½" x 1½" (B)
4 strips 3⅜" x 1½" (C).

Cut 1 strip ⅞" wide of black print.

From the strip cut 24 segments 1½" long (D).

Cut 1 strip 1½" wide of red stripe. From the strip cut 12 squares 1½" x 1½" (E).

Make 4 pieced Border 3 strips as shown, 2 for the sides and 2 for the top and bottom.

Add Border 3 to the quilt as shown.

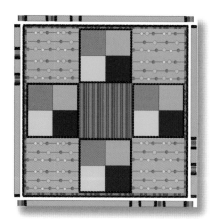

Finishing the Quilt

Quilting

Layer the quilt, batting, and backing. The batting and backing should be several inches bigger than the quilt on all 4 sides.

Quilt by hand or machine. Trim the batting and backing even with the quilt top.

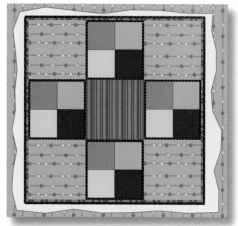

Binding

Cut 3 strips 2½" wide of black print and join end-to-end.

Press the binding strip in half lengthwise. Use this binding strip and your favorite method to bind the quilt. We prefer a mitered binding (page 17).

Monster Game Pieces

Cut 10 squares 12" x 12" of solid black for the appliqué bases.

Make all appliqués for the game pieces. (Refer to the **Easy OutLine Appliqué Technique**, pages 12–14.)

After making all the appliqués remove the paper backing from the fusible. Center the appliqués on the squares. Fuse in place following the manufacturer's instructions. Refer to the original pattern and photo for placement.

Layer the tic-tac-toe monsters with the batting and backing. Quilt each tic-tac-toe monster piece.

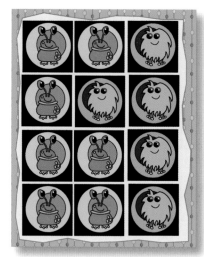

Finishing the Monster Game Pieces

After quilting, trim the monster game pieces to a circular shape cutting about ¼" away from the edge of the appliqués.

Cut a 36" x 36" square of black fabric to make the 2½" wide continuous bias binding (page 20).

Press the binding strip in half lengthwise and use to bind the monster pieces.

You're ready to play Tic-Tac-Toe.

Finished size 16" x 14"

Monster Tote Bag

REFERENCE INSTRUCTIONS

Easy OutLine Appliqué Technique

(page 12)

Read all instructions before starting.

MATERIALS

Tote Bag Background	Fat Quarter Red Stripe
	17" x 9" Green
Tote Bag Borders & Handles	¼ Yard Dark Blue
Monster Body & Legs	8" x 8" Turquoise
Monster Body	8" x 8" Red
Background	11" x 11" Purple
	4" x 6" Dark Blue
	8" x 8" Yellow
Monster Legs	4" x 6" Dark Purple
Spots, Eyes, Toes	4" x 6" Green
Eye Highlight	3" x 3" White
Appliqué Base	12" x 12" Solid Black
Paper-Backed Fusible Web	⅔ Yard
Backing	⅝ Yard Muslin
Batting	1 Yard
Lining	⅝ Yard Dark Blue

PREPARE THE APPLIQUÉ PATTERN by printing 24mnst_tote_fit.pdf from the ladybugpatterns folder on the CD.

Select Fit to Printable Area from the Page Scaling drop down menu. (See detailed printing instructions, pages 21–22.)

Tape the pages together according to the diagram. Trim the excess white border from adjoining pages as necessary.

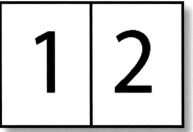

Tote Bag

- Cut 2 rectangles 17" x 7½" of red stripe.
- Cut 2 strips 17" x 1" of dark blue.
- Cut 1 rectangle 17" x 9" of green.

Join the strips and rectangles as shown.

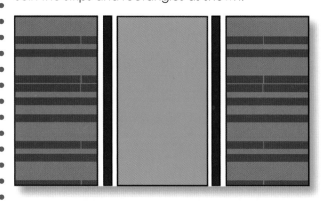

Appliqués

Make all appliqués for the tote. (Refer to the Easy Out-Line Appliqué Technique, pages 12–14.)

Remember that all appliqué patterns are printed in mirror image so they will be the same direction as the photo when the quilt is complete.

After making all the appliqués remove the paper backing from the fusible. Position and fuse in place following the manufacturer's instructions. Refer to the photo for placement.

The appliqué base looks like this.

Finishing the Tote Bag Quilting

Layer the appliquéd tote bag background, batting, and muslin backing. The batting and backing should be several inches bigger than the quilt on all four sides.

Quilt by hand or machine. Trim the batting and backing even with the tote top.

Cut a piece of lining fabric the same size as the quilted tote bag.

Handles & Side Seams

Cut 2 strips 24" x 4¾" of dark blue.
Cut 4 strips 24" x 1¾" of batting.

Press under ¼" along one long edge of each dark blue strip. Center 2 pieces of batting on each dark blue strip. Fold the raw edge over the batting and then the folded edge so it covers the raw edge. Stitch along the folded edge. Machine quilt straight lines about ¼" apart on the length of the handles.

Handles Step 1

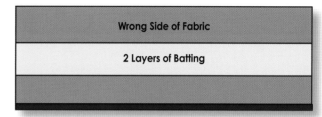

Handles Step 2
Raw Edge Folded Over Batting

Handles Step 3
Folded Edge Folded to Cover Raw Edge of Fabric

Handles Step 4
Lines of Stitching ¼" Apart

Center the handles 7" apart at both ends and baste the handles in place.

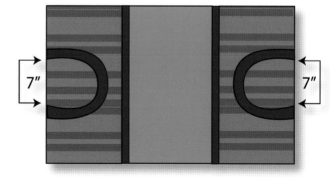

Fold the quilted tote in half, right sides together. Cut a 1½" x 1½" square out of the lower corners of the folded fabric as indicated by the dotted lines.

Sew the side seams of the tote bag. The arrows in the diagram indicate the seams.

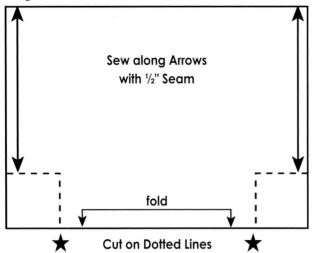

Sew along Arrows with ½" Seam

fold

Cut on Dotted Lines

Fold the cut-out corners shut by matching the side seams with the center of the tote bottom as indicated by the stars. Stitch the raw edges together with a ½" seam. Turn the tote right-side out.

Lining

Fold the lining in half, right sides together. In the same way, cut a 1½" x 1½" square from the lower corners of the folded fabric.

Stitch one side seam and a partial side seam (indicated by the arrows) with a ½" seam allowance, leaving an opening for turning the finished tote right-side out.

Fold the cut-out corners shut, matching the stars to the side seams. Stitch the raw edges together with a ½" seam.

Leave the lining inside out with the seams on the outside.

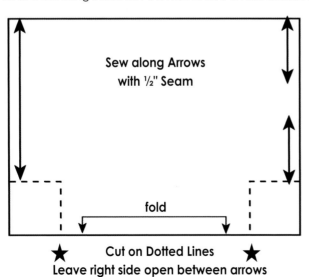

Sew along Arrows with ½" Seam

fold

Cut on Dotted Lines
Leave right side open between arrows

Place the tote inside the lining, right sides together. Match the side seams and pin together around the top edge.

Sew the tote and lining together at the top edge with a ½" seam allowance. Pull the tote through the opening in the lining. Tuck the lining inside the tote, pushing the lining corners into the corners of the tote and folding the lining over the quilted edge of the tote. This will leave ½" of the lining showing along the top edge of the tote.

On the outside of the tote, stitch in the ditch along the seam joining the lining and the quilted tote, folding the handles up out of the way of the stitching.

Pull the handles up into the correct position to carry the tote and topstitch in place.

Blindstitch the opening in the lining closed.

The tote is complete.

MEET THE AUTHORS

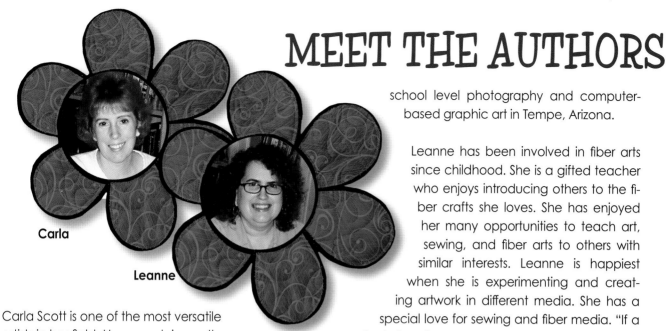

Carla

Leanne

school level photography and computer-based graphic art in Tempe, Arizona.

Leanne has been involved in fiber arts since childhood. She is a gifted teacher who enjoys introducing others to the fiber crafts she loves. She has enjoyed her many opportunities to teach art, sewing, and fiber arts to others with similar interests. Leanne is happiest when she is experimenting and creating artwork in different media. She has a special love for sewing and fiber media. "If a technique involves thread in any way, I am interested in doing it."

Carla Scott is one of the most versatile artists in her field. Her porcelain, earthenware, and glass designs are truly exquisite and unique. Known for her vivid and vibrant colors, Carla creates dimensional boxes, multi-layered decorative giftware, and various other designs. She has been working with ceramics for over 30 years, in glass and glass fusing for the past 15 years, and is now quilting.

Carla combines her experience and skill in ceramics and glass with her passion for color and fabric as she co-creates designs for Quilted Frog. She has designed and produced items for her former company, Clay Castle, her partnership in Studio Designs, and now her own company, Designs By Carla. Carla has also produced gallery pieces for Warner Brothers Stores and items for Disney catalogs and parks. Each piece is painstakingly handled from concept to completion, requiring much handling along with multiple firings. Each piece is hand created and painted with fine detail. Whether she is designing a piece for Designs by Carla or someone else, Carla Scott enjoys the process of creating. She states, "Even in my free time I am always doing watercolor or acrylic paintings. I love the creative process and everything involved with it."

Leanne Smith has an extensive fine arts background and holds a BFA in photography. She works in black-and-white photography and digital imaging. Her narrative style often employs groups of images used to express complex ideas. For many years she and her husband ran a photography studio as well as printing for other studios. In 2001, Leanne earned an MEd in curriculum and instruction. She now teaches high-

Both sisters have been sewing from the age of ten. They studied sewing in junior high, high school, and college. In 2000, Carla caught the quilting bug and has been busy designing, making, and teaching quilting ever since. Leanne began quilting over 30 years ago while still in high school. In 2003, Carla and Leanne decided to work together designing quilting patterns. They both love the idea of creative art and have fun with whimsical quilt subjects and bright colors, which are just their cup of tea. So they named their company Quilted Frog and the adventure began.

Carla and Leanne have designed and produced many quilt patterns and have been vendors at the Houston Quilt Market since 2003. As Quilted Frog has expanded, Carla has become an expert longarm machine quilter. They have won several awards for their designs and longarm quilting as well as having several quilt designs published in magazines.

They've had a lot of fun the last few years. Keep watching! Carla and Leanne have lots of new ideas for this year. They hope you will enjoy collecting and making their cheerful designs to gladden your heart and home.

Browse their website at www.quiltedfrog.com to see their entire line of quilt and punch-needle designs and watch for the debut of their new machine embroidery designs.

OTHER AQS BOOKS

Here is just a small selection of the books available from the American Quilter's Society. AQS books are known worldwide for timely topics, clear writing and illustrations, and accurate patterns. The following books are available from your local bookseller, quilt shop, or public library.

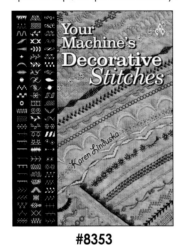

#8353

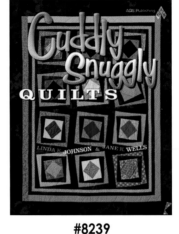

#8239

#8238

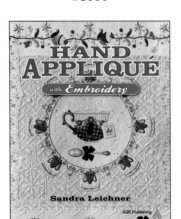

#8244

#8347

#8355

#8349

#8350

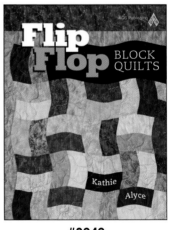

#8242

If you can't find these books, CALL or VISIT our website at

WWW.AMERICANQUILTER.COM

1-800-626-5420